MW00886587

Also by Maynard Kaufman

Adapting to the End of Oil: Toward an Earth-Centered Spirituality : 2008

The Organic Movement in Michigan (ed.) : 2017

From James Joyce to Organic Farming:

A Memoir

by Maynard Kaufman

Published by Helianthus Press
P.O. Box 361, Bangor, MI 49013

www.helianthuspress.com

ISBN: 978-1718818224

Library of Congress Control Number: 2018947026

Cover Illustration by Conrad Kaufman

Dedicated to my children:

Jonathan

Nathan

Karl

Conrad

Adrian

Who were sometimes enriched and sometimes inconvenienced by the seasonal arrival of homesteading students in our household. (For more details see first entry in “Notes and References.”)

Preface

As I shared what I was writing for this Memoir with my wife and sons, they reminded me, repeatedly, of other events that I failed to mention. My response was that this is not an autobiography but a memoir that deals only with the major issues that shaped my life as outlined in the table of contents. The second part of my response was that I had already written a sort of autobiography in 2011 which I called *Autobiographical Fragments*. It was almost 200 pages in length and included stories of my boyhood and youth, more details about family relationships, and more philosophical reflections, in addition to many of the topics included in this Memoir. I had it printed and bound and sent it to friends and relatives.

As I looked back on what I have written in this Memoir I think I have avoided making ultimate judgments about what I did with my life. I did not write to excuse my failures on a professional level as an academician. Nor did I write to justify that part of my life that led to my activities as an organic farmer. To begin with, I wrote because I thought the major decisions in my life, and their consequences, might be an interesting story. As the writing progressed I realized I was trying to articulate how my life was a moral response to the major environmental issues of our time. This effort was finally more self-conscious in the final chapter.

Readers are invited to make their own moral judgments of the life I have tried to portray, and I assume that will be determined by the values they cherish. I trust my values shine through the following text, and that I have not been too tiresome in explaining them. This writing has been a process of self-discovery.

Contents

Chapter I:
A Time of Transition

I will never forget that I grew up on a small farm in South Dakota during the drought and dust storms of the 1930s. There is much more to say about this, but what I learned was that, although I enjoyed growing up on a farm, farming was an undependable way to make a living. Like many a farm boy in that era, I left the farm to go to college and prepared to be a teacher.

I began my teaching career at Western Michigan University in 1963 and very soon I embodied the cultural changes that made the late sixties and early seventies a time of transition. The sixties were great years in which to begin teaching. Since I was the third person hired in the new Department of Religion, my colleagues and I had a very interesting and congenial time working out a new curriculum. Enrollments at Western were growing rapidly and there was an openness to new possibilities. The Honors College, under the direction of Sam Clark, started in those years and as Sam and I became friends I was able to teach courses in Honors nearly every year. Most of these were innovative and explored current topics. The counter-culture, with its permissive attitude toward any experimentation, was alive and well at WMU.

According to an entry in my journal, my wife Sally and I began thinking about starting some sort of free school, or a school of homesteading, in July of 1971. This idea was rooted in our experience on the first farm we bought at 9687 West M Avenue, near Oshtemo, Michigan. It cost $8,500, and was the first of many we looked at that we could afford. We intended to buy our own place, and I really wanted a place in the country. Although Sally was initially reluctant about this, she and the children agreed to give life in the countryside a try. We bought the farm in April of 1964 and by July we managed to get out of our one-year lease at 2155 Oakland Drive in Kalamazoo and move to the country.

The next few years were a time of incredible activity as I prepared my courses, repaired a run-down farm, entertained old friends from Chicago and colleagues from Western, planted fields and gardens and trees, repaired old barns and built new ones. An excerpt from my journal dated July 2, 1966, can illustrate this.

> I have sent the piece on J.F. Powers in to Pres Roberts and am now revising "Post-Christian Aspects of the Radical Theology" for a book to be edited by Thomas J. J. Altizer. I should be done with this in a couple of weeks and then only the dissertation remains. But in the meantime the hay will need to be cut in a couple of days—the oats are also starting to ripen too—and then it will take a few more days to rake and haul it in. I plan to stack it loose in the pasture. Later I have a little plowing to do too.

This mixture of work in my study and out in the field is typical, and I enjoyed the alternation.

One major project at this time was a complete renovation of the old part of the house and the addition of an enormous wing to it in 1967. This was done mostly with money Sally inherited when her father died. Our carpenter for the house was a former, or "fallen-away," Mennonite like me, named Sol Stucky, who had been a student of mine. His helper was my brother Roy, who as a student first at Goshen College and then at the Mennonite Seminary in Elkhart, visited us often. We all agreed to call the place *"Gnadenhof"* (yard of grace). After the house was finished and the work on the grounds began to bear fruit,

Sally and I fell in love with it and with our very active life on it. She had three or four well-planned and really showy flower gardens; I was very pleased with my gardens and the little barns I built.

In the late sixties living on the land did not threaten my academic career. I was at the height of my power, in my late thirties, with unbounded energy and enthusiasm. So I was able to rise rapidly in academia and also enjoy raising our food on a place we had made our own. Nor was life in the country considered a distraction from academia; many of my colleagues also tried it for shorter or longer times. Our place was also of great interest to my students, both because of the parties we hosted there, and because they were genuinely interested in growing food and living on the land. It is important to remember that the Sixties were the beginning of the back-to-the-land movement. So the students who wanted to help us raise food on the place on M Avenue generated the idea of a school of homesteading.

Several developments in 1970 led to a new emphasis in my career. I was appointed to the university-wide Committee on Environmental Programs and this led me to drop some literature courses and add courses on environmental topics. I was active on the sub-committee that developed the undergraduate curriculum for Environmental Studies, and later, in 1972, I was elected to chair the COEP. Also, as a Kent Fellow who fairly regularly attended the annual so-called Week of Work, I agreed to serve as the convener of the morning group discussion on the natural environment scheduled for late summer at Santa Cruz. I invited Paul Shepard, who later became famous as a more radical or "deep" ecologist, to lead the morning discussion group. So I became an "environmentalist" as environmental concerns were becoming mainstream. (Just how I became an environmentalist is explained in a later chapter.) It did not take me long to see that household food production with organic methods was better than industrial methods of food production in preserving ecological integrity. I was also increasingly concerned about energy use at this time; a concern I may have taken to extremes. I had been invited to a conference on ecology and religion at Claremont by John Cobb. I was planning to attend and even arranged for the University to pay my air fare. Then I thought about all that jet fuel that would be burned and the pollution it would create and canceled my plans to attend. This fixation on personal purity was certainly regrettable as it denied the important contacts that conferences made possible.

In 1971 I was granted a sabbatical leave, ostensibly to study rural communes and the eschatological aspects of the new youth culture. Toward that end Sally and I participated in a conference on communes near Antioch College at Yellow Springs, Ohio. We also attended the Week of Work at Aurora, New York, and came back through Canada to see former students in a commune. Finally we took a long trip through Wisconsin, South Dakota, Kansas and Missouri to visit communes and look for areas where farmland was inexpensive and attractive. We had vaguely been thinking about moving to set up some "free school" where various rural skills might be taught. This idea was reinforced by our reading about, and visiting with, rural communards who too often had no idea about how to raise food.

My cousin Roger was the only one in his Wisconsin commune with a farm background who knew anything and he held back out of respect for the communal ethos. In short, we saw the need for a school of homesteading.

In my book on the beginning of the organic movement in Michigan I did emphasize the importance of the back-to-the-land movement as it influenced the shape of the organic movement. This influence was also emphasized by other early leaders of the organic movement. Here is what Ronnie Cummins, the national director of the Organic Consumers Association, wrote:

> In the late 1960s, those of us coming out of the civil rights movement and the anti-war movement saw that building a counter-culture or an alternative economy was a political strategy for radical social change. We realized that protesting in the streets and even lobbying for civil rights legislation wasn't enough, and that we needed to have fundamental changes throughout the institutions. One of those things that started as a political tactic was to build food cooperatives all over the nation and have those communes, those back-to-the-land communes. This was really the impetus behind the modern organic, buy local movement. It was started with a political holistic vision.

This is a concise statement of how comprehensive the transition was at this time.

So in 1971 and 1972 we looked for a larger farm which would serve as the site for a school of homesteading. We seriously considered a place near Lawrence, then a place between Gun Lake and Shelbyville, and finally found the ideal place just north of Bangor, Michigan.

The move we were proposing came, ironically, at a time when my career was prospering. Promotions and increments in salary came rapidly. By 1968, in my fifth year at Western, I was promoted to Associate Professor with tenure and a salary of $9,100. I finally completed my dissertation on the writings of James Joyce and received my doctoral degree from the University of Chicago Divinity School in the fall of 1971. Although I did submit the dissertation for publication (unsuccessfully), I was more intensely excited by another essay I wrote and published at about the same time on "The New Homesteading Movement: From Utopia to Eutopia." This essay grew out of my sabbatical project and was reprinted a couple of times. The juxtaposition of the dissertation and homesteading is significant: the topic of homesteading reflected my activity of rebuilding the run-down farm at 9687 West M Avenue and, of course, our preliminary thoughts about a school of homesteading, live issues for us at the time in contrast to the dissertation on James Joyce.

I did publish several good essays in the late sixties on literary and theological topics, but farm work took precedence and kept me from writing more. One of these, "Post-Christian Aspects of the New Theology," was published in Thomas J. J. Altizer's book *Toward a New Christianity*, and attracted the attention of other theologians, such as Harvey Cox at Harvard, who listed it in one of his books among "Some Relevant Theological Currents." My "post-Christian" essay was considered as a radical and original approach to what other radical theologians were writing at the time.

As I look back I am amazed by how rapidly our plans for a school of homesteading became reality. From July in 1971 when my private journal records our first thoughts about the possibility of a school of homesteading to November of 1972 when we bought the farm near Bangor, was only 16 months. In summer of 1971 Sally and I made a longer trip looking for farms especially in Wisconsin and Missouri, but decided to maintain our connection to WMU. How could we have even considered leaving a paying job with three children to support? In retrospect, it seems that we nearly lost our sense of reality in the transition. We seemed to have been carried along by powerful cultural currents of which we were not fully aware, perhaps because we had internalized them and failed to see them objectively.

The academic year of 1972-73 was my last year of full-time teaching and a crucial year in my career. To begin with, I wrote a "Proposal for a School of Homesteading" and circulated it among friends and colleagues in the department in spring of 1972. Cornelius Loew, who had hired me and was now in an administrative position to approve or not, gave an informal approval for my half time leave of absence at half salary, but with full benefits. By this time my annual salary was around $12,000, nearly twice what it had been when I started at WMU nine years earlier. We knew how to raise our own food, so we were confident about being able to make a living on a half salary.

It may be worth noting that Cornie had his own reasons for approving my half-time leave of absence. We got along quite well and had both received Kent Fellowships in graduate school. It was with Kent Fellowship funding (then the National Council for Religion in Higher Education) that Cornie started the Religion Department at Western. Anyway, he had talked to me a little later, complaining that his son was being attracted by a cultish type of fundamentalism and hoping that a more neutral environment, as on our farm, would help the young man return to normality. We took the hint and included his son among our students in 1976.

One other issue Sally and I were concerned about was the relatively large amount we had to pay for income tax as my salary grew. We were strongly opposed to the war in Vietnam and wanted to avoid paying so much tax to support the war. This was another reason why we were happy to offer to work for a half salary. We had multiple motives.

In early fall of 1972 my colleagues in the Religion Department let me know that they wanted me to replace Tom Lawson as chair of the Department. My colleagues already knew that Sally and I were looking for a larger farm. But we met at Tom's house one evening to talk it over and I was almost willing to be convinced to do it. They may have wanted to keep me as a full-time faculty member in the Department. While I knew they were honoring me, I finally refused their offer, saying I wanted to start a School of Homesteading. Some were slightly offended by my refusal, but the meeting ended with mutual respect and good will all around. I think they recognized that I was following my heart and were able to respect that.

The School of Homesteading

Sally and I had been looking for the perfect farm for a School of Homesteading and felt we finally found it. It was 101 acres just north of Bangor with a big beech tree shading a large brick house in the Italian Revival style. It also had another smaller house, several barns, ponds, streams, and woods, and was bordered by the Black River at the back. I was very happy to have a real farm and dreamed pleasant dreams about it for years after we moved there.

We were able to pay cash for the farm at the closing on November 4, 1972, just a week after we sold the property at 9687 M Avenue. We felt it was a fated synchronicity: selling the old place for $46,000 and buying the new place for $45,000. The place we sold included a Farmall Cub tractor with various accessories and the place we bought included a Ford 8N tractor and other old tools. Soon after the closing we began moving things and building fences to contain the livestock we planned to move. The moving day was November 11 and with help from a number of students we got settled in the old brick house. At the end of our moving day we treated the students who helped us to pizza.

It was a slow supper since we strained the capacity of the local pizza place.

Soon after, we hosted a meeting on campus for people who might be interested in applying to the School of Homesteading. About 90 people showed up and many applied. We chose ten for the first class which started in spring of 1973. One of them, Greg Smith, probably the brightest

student I ever had and later a glass-blowing artist, came a couple of months early and helped us get the place ready for students. Most of these were from Western, but in subsequent years, after publicity in magazines with national circulation, we had students from other states and countries.

The School of Homesteading was a really decisive step in my teaching career and it is time to explore the many motives that prompted us to do it. It was clear to me that this was the next step in my environmental work, but the depth of my personal involvement suggests that other motives were present. Certainly my dissertation was finished and I was not ready for more book-writing. We had also finished our house-building and, as Sally and I sat in our living room (with white walls, red carpet and black furniture), we told each other, "Now we are living." The fact is that we were at the end of a major project and had no new project. We were a bit bored, perhaps in a mid-life crisis, and it affected both of us. Although I asked her repeatedly to be sure she was ready to leave her dream house, Sally never raised objections about the possibility of moving on. She considered herself a full partner in the School of Homesteading. She was pleased that students who visited us at the place on M Avenue valued her expertise in gardening and food preservation. We were both ready for a new project.

Self-provisioning in food was a central emphasis at the School of Homesteading. In fact we considered only the food we raised and processed at home to be "authentic." It was clear to me that small-scale organic farming and homesteading, with an emphasis on household food production, was energy-conserving and less polluting. It was also a way to counter predicted shortages of fossil fuel energy, which soon materialized in the OPEC oil embargo of 1973. These premonitions of oil shortages were reinforced by the "limits to growth" books published at about that time. Homesteading, we felt, was the wave of the future.

There were other motivations that could be called "spiritual." We were disillusioned with our commodity-intensive way of life with its shoddy consumer goods. We were ready for more "voluntary simplicity," for a way of life that would leave more time for leisure and reflection and non-material values. We shared the values of students who had "dropped out" and we were motivated to provide a place for students like these. According to our Proposal for a

School of Homesteading, "The ethos of the new homesteading movement thus involves a total reappropriation of oneself and one's world, and to this extent it depends upon a change as radical as a religious conversion." For me it involved a search for authenticity, for a way of life that was more genuine.

Another way of putting this is to say we were searching for a more integrated way of life, beginning with the integration of living and learning. In the "Proposal" I explained that an "alternative" suggests another or second birth, like a religious conversion, and I went on to explain:

> Perhaps I am even willing to run the risk of being misunderstood as a guru because of my feeling that we have too long perpetuated, in academia, a vicious dualism between mind and body, theory and practice, scientific detachment and emotional involvement, so that the strains imposed by these dualisms are reverberating throughout the entire ecosystem. In fact we are not disembodied spirits, but spirited bodies; as such we are not detached but involved with each other and with the total environment, not just in theory but in practice.

This holistic emphasis was also given clear expression in our homesteading brochure.

> The School of Homesteading is thus a place where theory and practice can come together. This kind of integration is also characteristic of a life lived close to the land, for in it production and consumption, way of life and means of livelihood, similarly come together. On a more general level, homesteading is a way of enlarging one's ecological awareness as it facilitates the integration of human beings with their natural environment.

Needless to say, these abstract descriptions did not always filter down to the level of everyday life. One of our first year students, who had taken my religion courses on campus, complained that the School of Homesteading was one of the most profane places he had experienced! He meant that it did not manifest conventional symbols of religiosity. I did bend over backwards to avoid the appearance of conventional religiosity—and to avoid looking like a guru.

I should add a slight qualification. Some of what I quoted above may have been more a rationale or justification for the school than a motivation. I was seriously dissatisfied with the state of education at the time, as I still am, and we tried to create a pilot project as an educational alternative which included hands-on experience. But the more general idea of integration may have been a motivation on a more personal rather than institutional level. In religious terms I suppose I was seeking my vocation, my calling.

Day to day activities at the School were more mundane. Except for the first year, when we had ten students in residence, there were eight in each class, four men and four women. The term began in April and ended after harvest activities were complete. This was usually in October, but some stayed longer to harvest firewood. We had regular classes in residence in 1973, 1974, 1976, 1977, and 1981. In 1975 we had groups of students for weekends only, and some returned for weekends throughout the season. 1978 was the first year of classes at the Land Trust Homesteading Farm (described below) and we managed without students on our farm. In 1979 we had only a married couple, and often in subsequent years we had only two or three students while the Land Trust Farm had more.

In earlier years we charged students in regular classes an entering fee of $300 of which we refunded $225 on a prorated basis during the latter half of the term. In the first year or two nearly all the students came from Western or from other areas in Michigan. In later years they came from further away, including from other colleges. In 1981 we had a young man from Germany and in 1985 another from Mexico.

We thought the flyer or brochure we distributed at the beginning of the course was clear and explicit about learning activities at the School. But because urban students had no context to imagine what we were talking about, they often complained that they did not understand what we were doing. As the years went by we aimed to be more and more explicit in describing what we did, but many prospective students were still mystified by the "curriculum." The simple truth is that we did what we needed to do in season in order to raise garden vegetables, field crops, and livestock. This was necessary so we could make the money we needed to live on, and, given that we made that money with farm activities, it was a realistic basis for the curriculum. Students usually understood this after a season on the farm.

A household of 15 or more people, including our children, required some careful planning and organization in order to function in an orderly manner. We usually divided students into "teams" who were responsible for doing things. The kitchen team of two persons worked on providing food for the group, usually for three day periods. Another team worked on milking cows and goats. Still others had responsibilities for other regular chores, such as care of other animals and poultry. Those who were not involved in regular chores or household work participated in ongoing farm and garden work. Sally and I exempted ourselves from these teams except that Sally was in regular consultation with the kitchen team. She also planned garden work, although eventually students could volunteer to be the "garden manager" for a period of time. I tried to figure out what other farm and field work needed to be done.

In the early years we tried to excuse students on Sundays while we did the work on that day. We also encouraged students to invite friends and relatives on Sundays only. But because Sally and I were also involved in Sunday activities and in regular Sunday potlucks, the plan for us do chores on Sundays was soon discontinued. The tradition of pot-luck dinners at noon on Sundays was a really successful development with our friends, both old and new, who also came to visit.

One of our attempts to make money was to raise vegetables in the field just south of the house. We called this the "commercial garden." The rows on it stretched for about 400 feet in an east-west direction. When students complained that the rows were too long I put a north-south lane in the middle to shorten the rows. The produce was harvested and displayed on an old wagon in a conspicuous place near the road for local people who drove by. Much of the produce was also taken to farmers markets in Kalamazoo and later in South Haven. A large share of this harvest was also consumed by those of us who lived on the

Two of our students at a farmers market

farm. In early years there was considerable emphasis on foraging for wild plants in fields and forests, but as our gardens expanded and small fruit was being produced, we found it more efficient to harvest what we planted. Since orchards took longest to get started we did depend on the wild apples that grew from seed in hedgerows on the farm for many years, along with mulberries.

As we were trying to get the School started we spent (or wasted) a great deal of time trying to teach in more areas than we had time for. In the first year we tried to introduce students to raising sheep, shearing the wool, spinning, making fabric and dyeing it with wild plants we gathered. This even involved field trips to visit people who actually did these things. Eventually our curriculum focused on raising food, preserving it, and preparing it to eat. Building projects, which emerged as we needed to prepare space for livestock, or building fences to contain livestock, did expand learning activities beyond food. Working in the woods to cut, split and gather firewood also took us beyond food.

Each year we also discovered that certain students already had mastered useful skills. In the first year George Williston built a 3 foot by 6 or 7 foot heavy duty work table for the kitchen out of a black walnut log we found. We left it in the kitchen when we sold part of the farm with buildings to the Arboreals and it is still in use. Other topics on homesteading skills were discussed rather than practiced, and we did set aside an evening each week for discussions, sometimes with special guests we invited for these occasions. Reading materials from our extensive library on homesteading were also recommended by us and usually ignored by the students who preferred to learn by oral tradition from Sally or me.

There were some activities that could be chosen by students as "electives," such as castrating baby pigs. Vegetarians could be excused from butchering chickens or animals. Students who had a special interest in something, such as beekeeping, or care of sick animals, could continue and develop that interest throughout the term. We rarely excused students from regular activities even though some were vastly uninterested in some things. Everyone had to care for farm animals. Everyone had to learn to drive the tractor and use farm machinery. I worked with each person on this and it required much patience on my part.

Mowing, raking, loading and unloading hay was a regular job on hay fields, which were mostly alfalfa and native grasses. Mowing was usually done with a sickle-bar

A hayloader in operation

mower mounted on a Farmall B tractor, a skill that was difficult for some to learn. Raking hay into windrows was easier and loading it on a wagon required a team of six persons in early years: one driving the tractor, one on the wagon laying the load, and two on each side forking the hay from the windrows onto the wagon. Unloading the wagon up into the hayloft was done with five or six grapple hook loads that were pulled up with the long hay rope and then dropped at the right place. In later years, when we worked with smaller groups or married couples, we got a hayloader and used it to load the hay over the back of the wagon. This required only one driver and one person on the wagon laying the load. And still later we got a hay baler (or several, until one actually worked). A grain elevator was used to take the bales up into the hayloft. Gradually, as we worked with fewer students we relied on more tractors and more mechanization. But we did learn that farm and garden work can be done easily with more people and fewer machines.

In earlier years I should have been using draft animals, like horses, which I grew up using on my father's farm. But horses were in greater demand during those back-to-the-land years of the 1970s; a team of horses cost a lot more than a small tractor, and we could not afford to buy horses. We did read the beautiful poem by Wendell Berry, called simply "Horses," instead.

The tractors came. The horses
stood in the fields, keepsakes,
grew old, and died. Or were sold
as dogmeat. Our minds received
the revolution of engines, our will
stretched toward the numb endurance
of metal. And that old speech
by which we magnified
our flesh in other flesh
fell dead in our mouths.

Wendell Berry

In 1974 our apprentices were joined by Jim Burgel who had some sort of scholarship to build a methane generator, or anaerobic digester. It cost us nearly a thousand dollars, but the publicity certainly made it a good investment. A field day devoted primarily to this project attracted around 300 visitors. And eventually the methane gas produced out of cow manure did replace purchased natural gas in our cook stove for short periods. We were able to switch the stove to biogas and there was enough produced in a day to cook lunch. Unfortunately, the cow manure slurry that was digested to produce the biogas was quite corrosive to the steel parts used to stir the slurry in the tank. So they rusted and did not last even a year. Jim Burgel learned to consider methane projects as "hot air for the press." Eventually the room that housed the methane generator became a milk room and housed the bulk milk tank instead.

Each class tended to generate its own *leit-motif* or characteristic theme. The group in the first year, harking

The class of 1973 and some of our children

back to the hippie concerns of the 1960s, generally expressed a revolutionary attitude. We never had serious conflicts about such political issues since we all shared aspects of it, but I recall one young woman muttering about "those goddam counter-revolutionaries," which may have referred, mistakenly, to my wife Sally. A man who was and remains a good friend of mine seriously proposed that we fly the black flag of anarchy on the old flag pole in the front yard, where our predecessors on the farm flew the American flag. I disagreed, and made sure that these long-haired rebels worked visibly in the garden along the road where they would demonstrate the good old-fashioned American work ethic for neighbors to see.

The second class, which included a young philosopher or two, got started on the possibility that this was not a "real" farm because it was organized for learning rather than for making money. Much debate followed about "reality" which those who wanted to get land compared to "realty." To those who failed to see irony when it was present, this class may have seemed far gone into ontological anxiety. Meanwhile, two young men from the Detroit area who were excellent musicians frequently entertained us and our guests. At about this time we promoted a policy of dinner potlucks on Sundays and it helped to keep our students on the farm. Our friends could also visit this "funny farm," and many did, along with many others who were curious about the School of Homesteading. Reporters often visited and wrote articles on how "college professor tries to bring back the good old days" and thus mythologized what I thought was a practical option.

The class of 1976, again balanced between four males and four females, all good-looking and strong, was one of the more normal groups we had. One of the women, Wendy, had applied to enter for a couple of years and her persistence paid off when Sally felt she should join us. Since her father was a military officer, she had lived in many places and was looking for a place to put down roots. She and Dennis, from Kentucky, told me one day that they were getting married at sunrise the next day under the big beech tree, and they did, but I failed to wake up in time. Later, thanks to Wendy's initiative, the class of 1976 was

The class of 1976

the only class to come back for a ten year anniversary. A larger reunion held in 1998 to celebrate 25 years was well attended.

By the time the class of 1977 came along our promotion of the School of Homesteading at Michigan State University, the Ag. School in Michigan, was bearing fruit. Three of the men were studying agriculture there and one in another college. So the focus that year was seriously vocational.

None of our apprentices over the years wanted to watch TV, and we didn't either, but this class had one person who wanted TV, so he had to set it up in one of the hay mows.

The last full size class included several unique people. Two young men were extremely athletic gymnastic artists who continually amazed the rest of us with their feats.

Given our legal liability, there were times when Sally and I did not want to know what they were doing, but somehow we got a photograph of Jake doing handstands on the top of the silo and on the peak of the barn roof. This was also the year when a young man from Germany joined us.

Developments After the School

The new emphasis on food and farming led to new activities in my life. I was an active participant in the formation of Organic Growers of Michigan, which was also organized in 1973. (More on this topic will be found in Chapter V.) Soon after articles appeared in magazines with national circulation—such as the one that featured our school in *Organic Gardening and Farming* in March of 1975—we had applications from potential students in other states. We were also contacted by an industrialist from Detroit, Joe Filonowitz, proposing that we start a land trust to provide land for our students. During the next year he and I incorporated Michigan Land Trustees as a tax-exempt organization after many meetings to make arrangements.

Soon after we started the School I had also begun planning how to get the University to offer courses on homesteading and had proposed that these courses be offered through the Environmental Studies Program. This required the writing of another proposal, soliciting the support of sympathetic colleagues, and countless meetings with administrators and with the Curriculum Committee in the College of Arts and Sciences. My proposal called for the University to pay a half-time salary to a Homesteading Instructor who would live on what we hoped would be a farm provided by the Land Trust and supervise the homesteading course as a living-learning experience. I was planning to offer a course called "Homesteading Theory" on campus. Given how unconventional homesteading was as a course of study and how complex the arrangement was, I was surprised and pleased when it was approved. The support of Cornie Loew, then Vice President for Academic Affairs, may have helped behind the scenes. But I was pleased that I still had credibility in the university community.

When Joe Filonowitz originally proposed the idea of a land trust as a business arrangement, in which it would acquire land by purchase or donation and lease it to young farmers, the Internal Revenue Service initially refused to approve it under Section 501(c)(3) of the IRS code. They suggested that our nascent organization should have an educational function to qualify as a non-profit organization. I was able to satisfy this requirement with my proposal for courses at Western. So in a remarkable synchronicity, the land trust made the homesteading courses possible and the homesteading courses made the land trust possible. Approval by the IRS allowed Joe Filonowitz to buy a farm across the street from ours and donate it to Michigan Land Trustees. So MLT became a reality and is still active after forty years. The arrangement I engineered continued for about five years until a new administrator at Western terminated its support for the homesteading program. After that the homesteading courses were supported by Michigan Land Trustees and continued for a few years.

Courses in Homesteading were so unique that the university seemed reluctant to delete them from the catalog. I had retired in 1987, but as late as 1991 a student transferred to Western to take the courses. We invited him to the Land Trust Homesteading Farm.

When considered in conventional terms, my academic career was radically altered and perhaps badly damaged by my digression to a School of Homesteading. Jerome Long, one of my best friends in the Religion Department, had warned me that “the university will chew you up and spit out the bones" if I went ahead with the School. He was partly right. I had no time (nor inclination) for writing and did not publish anything "academic" between 1972 and 1984, although I did publish many short articles and reviews for local newsletters such as those of Organic Growers of Michigan and Michigan Land Trustees. Meetings of OGM and MLT replaced AAR and SVHE (American Academy of Religion and Society for Values in Higher Education) conferences. When I was eligible for promotion to full professor I applied. The departmental promotion committee recommended my promotion by a vote of two to one, but I was not promoted because the vote had to be unanimous. Those who voted for my promotion credited my academic achievements, including the new homesteading courses on campus and the fact that I was written about more than any of my colleagues. I had huge scrapbooks of clippings of articles about our School, but promotion was apparently for published research only.

In 1979, my friend Ken Dahlberg from Political Science and I developed a new course, "Introduction to Appropriate Technology" and it was approved for the Environmental Studies Program. He had just published a book he titled "Beyond the Green Revolution" which was a well-documented critique of how the political and economic powers used emerging agricultural technologies for rural development in Third World countries. Along with critics of technology such as E. F. Schumacher and Ivan Illich, the Dahlberg book provided the conceptual basis for our new course. We team taught the new course with a fellow from the College of Engineering as the third person on the team. My contribution focused on household food provision strategies based on organic methods. It was a successful course and attracted some excellent students. Thom Phillips was one of the students in the course; he and I were able to put much of what we learned into practice when he agreed to build our off-grid house.

Ken Dahlberg and I shared a common interest in agriculture and food, along with more general environmental issues. We were both on the committee that developed the Environmental Studies Program. After Joe Filonowitz and I got Michigan Land Trustees started, Ken joined the board and then served as chairman for many years. Later we traveled together to national conferences on food and agriculture issues. Although Ken was in Political Science and I was in Religion, for many years we had offices in the same building and developed a close friendship.

The success of our new course emboldened me to seek funds for the establishment of a Center for Appropriate Technology and Homesteading on campus. Although I initiated the proposal and did most of the writing for it, I did get others from various colleges in the University to contribute to the proposal so it would be seen as a full-scale university program. We had tentative approval for a tract of land across the street from the small college farm that Western maintained. The proposal was sent to a federal program called "The Fund for the Improvement of Post-Secondary Education," and our preliminary proposal was accepted. We were asked to prepare a final proposal on which I spent many more hours. Then, when administrative people finally looked at our proposal and saw that it would cost the university about $4,000 and a small piece of land, they withdrew their support even though the university might have gained $200,000 for the new program and its buildings.

I was extremely crushed and disappointed and, in an entry in my Journal at about this time, when I was about 50 years old, I complained about being weary, tired, often sick, and yearning to retire. The Homesteading Practice course on the Land Trust Farm was no longer attracting enough students. The back-to-the-land and homesteading movements seemed to be declining. And I was harried with administrative details for which I was not paid. It was part of my task, among other things, to make arrangements for the hiring and salary of the Homesteading Instructor, but everything I decided had to be cleared with various administrators.

(Of course it did not occur to me at the time that the depth of my depression was a measure of how successful my experimental ventures up until then had been.)

The only thing I enjoyed was farming, or so I wrote in my Journal. I recall I was plowing one evening; the weather was balmy, the soil was moist and in good tilth, and I remember feeling I could do that for the rest of my life. I was sorely tempted to resign from teaching just then.

In spite of a few difficulties and disappointments, in retrospect I feel more positive than negative about the impact that the School of Homesteading had on my life and thought. I certainly can affirm the gratification I gained from working closely with students to open more holistic possibilities for them. A reunion of homesteading students after 25 years, in 1998, confirmed the fact that my efforts were deeply appreciated. This reunion was planned by some former students still in the area, by my wife Barbara, and especially by my stepson, Jon Towne, who ended up as the main instructor at the Land Trust Farm, a place he and his wife Bobbie Martindale eventually purchased as their own place.

Reunion of Homesteading students in 1998

I also enjoyed some favorable attention from the larger university community as a person who was willing to "walk his talk." Many faculty members attended our Sunday potluck dinners and over 70 showed up for a special open house we scheduled. As stated above, the School was also good copy for newspaper and magazine articles and Sally compiled several scrapbooks of such material. My efforts to create an educational alternative certainly generated more publication than that produced by most of my colleagues in the department. Unfortunately, my more than half-time absence from the Religion Department meant that I lost the close friendships I had enjoyed with colleagues during the years when the Department was getting started.

Above all, I value the ways in which the Homesteading "digression" (which may have been my true vocation and defined my career) opened me to new areas of inquiry. The idea of homesteading and self-provisioning led me to study and think and write about the informal economy as opposed to the money or market economy, a large and somewhat neglected area of inquiry. This also led me to the thought of Ivan Illich who was and remains an extremely important influence on my thinking as he challenged econocentric cultural assumptions and the disastrous "enclosure of the commons." His *Deschooling Society* reinforced my nascent critique of schooling directed exclusively to the head.

My participation in organic and sustainable farming and food production, in practice on the farm as well as on an organizational level, led me to a new interest in writing papers for academic conferences. From my background in literature I was able, for example, to relate the pastoral ideal to homesteading and sustainable agriculture. As a result I began attending academic conferences with my friend Ken Dahlberg and published a new series of articles on these topics. (More details will be found in the chapter on organic farming.) Finally, in 2003, I was able to relate issues in food production directly to religion in a short article entitled "Food Systems: Sacred, Profane and Demonic" (see Chapter VI).

Although we continued accepting a few homesteading students throughout the 1980s and 1990s, 1981 was the last year we had a larger group, consisting of about six students. In retrospect, it is clear that the 1970s were the back-to-the-land decade. Sally was a full partner in the School of Homesteading and, in spite of having her house invaded each spring by eight young people, she accepted and affirmed what we were doing. After she died in 1990, I was very fortunate to find another beautiful and intelligent woman, Barbara Geisler. She had grown up in Watervliet, a few miles southwest of Bangor, but left Michigan after college and lived in San Francisco for twenty years. When she returned to Michigan we met through a Green Politics group I had started. We were married in 1991. Working on the farm was not easy or natural for her, but she tried hard to adjust to it. Her efforts in helping to supervise apprentices made it possible to continue the School for another few years, and as I got older it was good to have helpers. After we met we remembered that she had been a student in the first religion and literature course I taught at Western, "The Religious Quest in Modern Literature."

Barbara and I, just married

In the 1980s my research shifted to apocalyptic and utopian topics which were already implied in my essay on the homesteading movement. I taught more courses on this topic, both in Religion and in the Honors College. I applied for and received sabbatical leave for the 1983-1984 school year to continue research and writing for a book I was calling "Visions of a New Earth." These visions were implied or found in utopian and/or apocalyptic expressions in contemporary culture. The long paper I wrote was on the nuclear peril and its apocalyptic implications. This is the time when Jonathan Schell's book, *The Fate of the Earth* was generating a lot of interest as it focused attention on the nuclear threat. After refining the prospectus for the book I spent several years sending it to many publishing houses. There was strong interest from an editor at the University of California Press, who happened to be Ernest Callenbach, author of *Ecotopia.* I had some communication with him earlier when he agreed to serve on the editorial board for a magazine or quarterly that Ken Dahlberg, Paul Gilk and I were planning. We proposed calling it *Eutopian Journal.*

But when Callenbach actually read a chapter he wrote back saying they did not have a religion editor at that time. Despite his strong interest, therefore, no offers were made to publish the book. Over half of the projected chapters in the book were already written. I was chastened by these rejections and began to doubt the validity of the book's thesis—that apocalyptic anxiety in a culture leads to the transformation of utopia into eutopia, to the search for a good place on the land, in nature, rather than the regimented "noplace" of classical technological utopias. I had to recognize the possibility that it was not a publishable thesis. Easily discouraged by rejection, I gave up.

My files show that after this I began writing more letters to administrators in defense of the liberal arts and in protest against the gradual transformation of the university into a glorified trade school useful to corporate America for job training. Yes, homesteading was a kind of job training too, but in a more holistic context, and it was this context for which I was arguing. On campus I was feeling increasingly discouraged and frustrated because the courses I wanted to offer did not attract enough students. I even went back to teach more courses in Religion, including the infamous Religion 100, an academically irresponsible survey of world religions that we offered to boost enrollments. But I was bored and no longer felt enthusiastic about doing a good job.

Back on the farm, I began planning to make it more profitable as I planned for retirement. With my son Conrad's help, in the summer of 1980, I began modifying the barn to set up a grade A dairy to provide the income we would need without a teaching job. Eventually, toward the end of 1986, I applied for retirement. The early retirement incentive payment was generous, and I was claiming full retirement benefits even though I had been on a half-time leave of absence for over half of my career. The payment, which included unused sick leave, was about four times my annual half-salary, but I felt I had earned it. I was able to buy a new Deutz 65 horsepower tractor, more land, and still have another small retirement fund.

One measure of my distance from University events was my disinterest in ceremony. I did serve on the Faculty Senate now and then, and served on some University-wide committees, but I had never participated in faculty processionals with cap and gown. When my son Conrad graduated, in my final year of teaching, I did intend to march in the processional. But then I forgot to order my cap and gown in time to participate.

When the university faculty chose to become a union for purposes of collective bargaining, I realized that teaching was a job much like any other. Earlier I had been thinking of it in more glorified terms as a profession, or as a career in which one succeeds or fails. I have come to understand that this was a mistake; everyone succeeds in some things and fails in others. I was no different. In this context promotion is of special value to those who seek to make more money. Since I always had some scruples about making money (and paying war taxes) I did not shed tears when I was not promoted to full professor. In fact, college professors are extremely desirous about making money. My colleagues were surprised when I was willing to forgo the raise that would have been mine if I had accepted the job of being chair. Later, I once suggested that instead of merit pay it might be better if we would be given time off instead. No one in the department agreed. And after one of my best friends in the department had a heart attack and I urged him to teach only half-time, he insisted on full time for the sake of bigger Social Security payments. Of course he died before he could collect them.

Although I took the path less traveled I was able to find my own way through the academic wilderness and I gained the esteem of some colleagues in the larger university community. My friendships with Environmental Studies faculty were and remain very special to me. The fact that I am still estranged from my former colleagues in Religion shows how deep the shift to my new vocation had been.

Chapter II: Back to the Farm

I say "back" to the farm partly because I grew up on a farm, about which I will write more in the next chapter. And of course we had the farm we built up at 9687 West M Avenue but, in contrast to the farm we bought near Bangor, it was a rural residence in a suburb of Kalamazoo. The farm to which we moved in November of 1972 was, in my judgment, a "real" farm, and it was the fulfillment of my long-term dream to have a "real" farm. After we settled here I repeatedly came back to this farm in my dreams at night, and they were always pleasant dreams. Although in my dreams I approached the farm and house from different directions and in different contexts, it was always the same old brick house. And in my dreams it was also a pleasure to explore the large barns, with their many lofts, pens, and passageways, and see the cattle contentedly chewing their cud.

While the several barns satisfied me that this was a real farm, it was the big brick house, shaded by an immense beech tree, that really stimulated my imagination when I first saw the farm. The house was built in the Italian Revival style with a roof that was almost flat. Inside, the house had many rooms: a large living room, dining room, kitchen, foyer at the front entrance, a bedroom or study, and, at the back door, a hallway we used as a canning kitchen. Beyond that was still another room used as a bedroom. Upstairs were four bedrooms and a bathroom. Downstairs the bathroom needed some finishing, which I promptly accomplished. The full Michigan basement had room for a laundry, a room to store canned goods, and a large furnace room with storage space for firewood.

And we loved showing the house. Local people who stopped by were always glad to be invited into the house and saw it as a long-deferred opportunity: "I've always wanted to see the inside of this house." We felt privileged to be living in it for thirty years.

The farm we bought was in Section 6 of Arlington Township in Van Buren County. Given how sections are numbered in townships, Section 6 was in the northwest corner of the township. The address of the house was 26041 County Road 681, just north of Bangor. It was said to include 101 acres but may have included a little more. Although there is a legal description, a graphic description might make more sense. The Black River is the meandering boundary in the back and as it changed course it could add or subtract acres. County Road 681 was along the front, or west side; and the City of Bangor was the boundary along the south. Later, in 1984, I was able to buy another 60 acres adjacent to the north boundary from my friend Joe Filonowitz, with whom I had organized Michigan Land Trustees.

Moreover, the house and farm had a long history. The 75 page abstract of title that we received when we bought the farm showed that Andrew J. Hull bought the basic 80 acres of the farm, along with 8.72 acres west of the Black river in the next 80 to the east, from H. S. Sanford on November 31 of 1869, but there was no other information about Andrew J. Hull. The abstract actually begins with the acquisition of the farm by John Lynch in 1896. We gleaned many details, often contradictory, about the house and the farm from the many descendants of John Lynch who visited over the years to say that they used to visit the place. Our garrulous neighbor, a junk dealer who knew John Lynch's son, Frank, told many stories about Frank and his drinking problem, and it all added to the romance of the farm. And while we knew that John Lynch did not build the house, for many years we did not know who did.

The Hull family in front of the house in about 1886.

The uncertainty of who actually built the house was clarified for us when Lee and Laurie Arboreal, to whom we sold the farmstead and some of the land, received a letter and some photos of the brick house early in 2012 from Greg Hull, who said he was the great grandson of A. J. Hull. Greg Hull explained that his great grandfather built the house in 1885 to 1887, and Greg sent some photos with people in nineteenth century garb standing in front of the house. Andrew J. Hull is the tall man with a dark beard standing near the center of the picture with his wife in a white blouse at his right side. This photo, probably from about 1886, also shows that the house was not yet finished. The steps that go down from the front doors in the northwest and southwest corners to the west now go down to the north and south. And a new front door, which does not appear in this photograph, was added near the center of the house.

After I wrote to thank Greg Hull, he sent me a great deal of information and specifically asked for more pictures of the interior of the house. I sent those to him, along with photos of other farm buildings, including the run-down old house in which the Hulls may have lived until the brick house was built. Greg replied by sending more legal data about the farm. He also sent information about H. S. Sanford, an investor and world traveler who had been appointed ambassador to Belgium (1861-1869) by President Lincoln. It is not likely that he ever lived on the land that he sold to A. J. Hull. And since there is no record of other owners, the Hull family were likely the first European family to live on this farm.

According to the information that Greg Hull sent me, Andrew J. Hull needed $2,600 to build the house, a sum which he borrowed from Edward Strong in Kalamazoo in 1885. Hull made a patent medicine and probably hoped that the money he made from that would enable him to repay the loan. But he was unable to repay that loan and as a result, according to Greg Hull, the house and farm was sold on the courthouse steps in Paw Paw in December of 1894 for $4,300. For some reason this detail is not recorded in the Abstract of Title that came with the land when I bought it. In any case, the Hull family was able to enjoy the new house only about eight years, although they lived a total of 26 years on the farm.

John and Charlotte Lynch bought the farm from Edward Strong in 1896, and they and their daughters owned it until 1961. In 1912 John Lynch also bought 11.47 acres to the south of the house for $1,500, which is now in the Bangor city limits. The three Lynch daughters sold the farm, now roughly 101 acres, to the Ciszewski family from Chicago in May of 1961. Sally and I bought it from them in November of 1972.

Buildings on the Farm

An important consideration for us as we planned for a School of Homesteading was a second house, which we called the tenant house, about a block north of the main house. During the first year it housed six students while we found room for four more on the first floor of the big house. In a year or two we moved a small house next to the tenant house so that there was ample room for all the students there. A blueberry grower, who had used the small house to house migrant workers, donated it to us. We moved it by jacking it up high enough to get a flat bed hay wagon under it and pulled it home.

The barns that were on the farm were adequate to start with, but we added more as our activities required more specialized space. The main barn, across the yard from the

The barns seen from the roof of the house

house, was a timber-framed structure of about 36 by 56 feet. It was very likely older than the house and still in fair condition but with some rotten beams. We spent time and effort to reinforce weak braces and prop up sagging beams. By adding sheds on the south side (first for the anaerobic digester and later for the milk room) and on the east side, (for a 20 foot wide loafing shed when we began a dairy), the barn was propped up to some extent. Of course I made sure the vertical boards that covered the outside were securely nailed. A steel track attached under the apex of the roof was useful for unloading hay. The ladders that were attached to upright beams to provide access to the top of the haymow seemed strong but at first I worried that they might no longer be strong enough to use. But they remained strong enough for the thirty years that I used them. The hay lofts were on each side of the ground level, but built up four feet higher to provide room for cattle below.

The 28 x 40 foot "horse" barn was offset to the south between the house and main barn. We used it as a shop because we did not have horses. I thought it might have been built fairly recently because it had 2 x 6 studs and was covered with horizontal drop siding, but it was visible on one of the early house photos from about 1887 and must have been at least that old. Like the main barn it had a hayloft about 20 feet high, but the hay door was nailed shut so we used it for baled hay, after adding more posts to support the floor of the hay loft.

Across from the horse barn and offset to the north between the house and main barn was a granary about 16 x 26 feet with an attached shed and corn crib. After patching the mouse holes in the grain bins we made use of them for storing grain. The second floor of the granary was used for storage and for craft activities. Just west of the granary and closer to the house was the chicken barn of about 12 x 32 feet. I made a partition wall in it so a part of it could be used for baby chicks and the other part for old hens. Since there was no floor in it we poured concrete for a floor, using sand from a pit on the field across the railroad tracks.

Just north of the hen house was an old building with remnants of wallpaper on the walls. We assumed it was once a house; it also had a nice stairs to the second floor. It was most likely the first house built by A. J. Hull when

Original home of the Hull family

they moved onto the farm, likely in 1869 or soon after. It was very run-down and the roof leaked so badly that we tore it down in about 2000, unaware then that it was the original home of the Hull family. Until then we used it as a goat barn.

There were also a couple of concrete-block silos near the barns that were originally used to feed the cattle. Since I did not have equipment for harvesting silage I did not use them. One of my stepsons did try to make an apartment in one of them, but mostly we enjoyed watching the bats come out of holes in the concrete blocks at twilight. We counted

90 one evening, and they ate mosquitos, so we welcomed them.

When were these buildings built, and by whom? We now know that the Hull family bought the farm in 1869 and that they most likely lived in the building we used as a goat barn until the big brick house was built in 1885 to 1887. It

Aerial view of the farm in the mid-1980s

is my theory that Andrew Hull built all the barns referred to above sometime between 1869 and 1884, most likely during the 1870s. The so-called horse barn, which I thought was of more recent vintage, shows its roof just beyond the house in one of the photos.

Thinking about these buildings in the past enhances their mythic power. But in reality the house was old and drafty, cold, and hard to heat in winter. It had high ceilings, nine feet and eight inches from the floor, with many transoms above the doors. We had insulation blown into the walls and installed storm windows. But the house had thirteen outside doors, four of them to little porches on the second floor, and there was not much we could do to keep the heat inside. Greg Hull mentioned that his great grandfather was a skilled craftsman who enjoyed building doors and windows. That may explain why he built thirteen doors to the outside. Although we burned ten to twelve full cords of firewood in the basement furnace, a gas stove was needed for supplemental heat. Soon we bought a combination kitchen stove with one half burning wood and the other half burning gas. It helped to warm the kitchen. The house was in the Italian Revival style of the 1880s and obviously not designed for Michigan winters.

The fairly flat roof was also not designed for Michigan rains. It had many leaks, both before and after we hired a young contractor to install a new steel roof. The leaks weakened the plaster on the ceilings, and an overnight guest once suffered an unpleasant awakening when plaster from the ceiling fell on her. Eventually many ceilings had to be rebuilt with new plaster. It is to the credit of the Arboreals that they took a major and expensive step toward preserving the house by totally replacing the roof, rebuilding it so that the roof is steeper and sheds rain properly.

When we moved to the farm the water supply was provided by the city of Bangor. The first water bill we received was about $400, so we assumed there were some leaky water pipes. We called a well-driller and got a new well of our own, and its water was excellent and plentiful. There was evidence of a well and a windmill on the north side of the house, but it was next to the old sewer system. The new sewer system we installed also went north of the house. Over the years as we added water lines to the outbuildings we figured out that we were adding the third water system on the farm. Once, as our homesteading apprentices dug a ditch for a new water line to one of the old barns, we were ready to connect the faucet to the new water line when we discovered that that old barn already had water through the old pipes. After all that unnecessary digging I was very unpopular for a few days.

When I rewired the electrical system in the house I discovered that I was adding the third system there too. The first was pipes for natural gas lighting; the second was an old wiring system with single wires on knobs and spools; while I was installing a three-wire grounded system with steel boxes. Needless to say, very few outbuildings had electricity, so they also needed wiring.

Although the house was occupied just before we moved in, the outbuildings had not been used for many years except by wild animals. During our first winter, a bitch had puppies under the granary, which was located between the house and the barn. Each time we walked by the bitch came out snarling in the most menacing manner. I was able to face her down and chase her back under the building, but children were terrorized as the bitch came toward them. We called the animal control officer in the county and he came out and sympathized, but said it was too dangerous to crawl under the building to kill the dogs. After he left I found a place where I could see under the granary and shot the bitch and most of her puppies. My son Conrad reminded me that we saved one puppy for our farm dog. This is as close as we got to the conquest of nature. Most of our efforts were intended to restore fertility to the fields.

In the summer of 1980, as I looked ahead to retirement, I got serious about developing another source of income. Conrad and I spent much of that summer building a loafing shed along the east side of the barn. I really appreciated his help that summer because I knew I could trust him in the difficult parts of the construction more than anyone else. We had no apprentices that summer anyway.

A loafing shed is a place where cattle can eat hay from mangers along the side closer to the existing barn and where they can sleep in separate stalls along the opposite side. These stalls were sized for Holstein cows, about 44 inches wide, and we were able to fit 14 of them in the 56 feet that were available. We also added four more stalls in the north part of the barn. The stalls were about four inches higher than the floor, bedded with straw, and sloped a bit down to the rear of the cow. They were designed to keep the cows cleaner, and they did. Most of their manure

Building the loafing shed

was dropped in the center alleyway of the loafing shed where it was easy to scoop up with the front end loader on the tractor.

The framework of the stalls supported the east side of the loafing shed roof, and the wall of the existing barn supported the west part, which was much higher. In between we built another support which consisted of fairly straight tree trunks. These served as the basis for a manger into which hay could be dropped from openings higher up in the hay barn wall to feed the cows. We toe-nailed the bottoms of the tree trunks to a 2 by 8 on the floor and then tied the tree trunks so they leaned away from the barn a bit. Then we each climbed two sixteen foot ladders tied at the top to make a stepladder, and I notched the tops of the tree trunks with a small chain saw so we could nail 2 by 10 supports to them for the rafters of the roof. After the supports were all in place and the rafters were nailed in place, the rest of the building process was easy. Then we mixed and poured a lot of concrete for the floor until we got tired and had the floor completed with concrete delivered by a truck. The concrete we poured was made with sand from our gravel pit and most of the dimension lumber was milled from tulip tree logs we cut in our woods.

Fields, Soils, and Woods

When we moved to the farm, nearly all the fields on the farm were hay fields in the process of reversion to native grass. Some had been abandoned several years before we came on the scene and were in the process of succession to forest. But the trees were still small enough to pull out with the small gray tractor, an 8N Ford that came with the farm. So we had a taste of clearing the land before it could be put into field crops. But it may have been wiser to follow the example of Wendell Berry as related in an untitled poem he wrote recently and collected in a little book called *Leavings.*

I go by a field where once
I cultivated a few poor crops.
It is now covered with young trees,
for the forest that belongs here
has come back and reclaimed its own.
And I think of all the effort
I have wasted and all the time,
and of how much joy I took
in that failed work and how much
it taught me. For in so doing
I learned something of my place,
something of myself, and now
I welcome back the trees.

Wendell Berry

Eventually the fields suitable for cropping were tilled and produced crops for us. Earlier, when I was starting out, I tilled the fields close to the hedge rows. Now, I too, let the trees encroach on the fields and even plant more trees to widen the hedge rows.

The soil types were excellent for field crops. The main soil type was Riddles, with sandy loam for the first foot or so down and heavier clay further down that helped to retain moisture. Other soil types associated with Riddles were also present: Capac, with heavier clay, and Selfridge, which was on the sandier side. I did not know this when I bought the farm. The soil survey of the county was not published until about ten years after we bought the farm. I probably bought the farm because I liked the big brick house shaded by that enormous beech tree and hoped the soil would be productive, as I assumed it was because the builder of the house could afford to build it. Of course it turned out that the builder of the house and the first farmer was more a jack of all trades who dabbled in the ministry and made a patent medicine. But the soil was very productive.

The railroad track between Grand Rapids and Chicago bisected our property from northeast to southwest with most of the good fields to the west of the railroad. These fields had both names and numbers. The number of the field indicated the acres in it as measured by the Soil Conservation Service, such as, for example, 6.8. The name of this field was North Dakota because it was the north field in a series of four that were laid out horizontally. So these fields were North Dakota, South Dakota, Nebraska and Kansas. Access to these fields was to the east of a lane that went straight north from the pond behind the barn. The 16 acre field east of these and across the railroad tracks was called Ohio, Sally's home state, so I could make a joke about her being born on the wrong side of the tracks. The fields south of the four horizontal fields were called Texas and New Mexico, while the fields to the west were called California and Ecotopia.

When we added 60 acres along the north side of North Dakota in 1984 we naturally had to call it Canada. The large 17 acre field on the northeast corner of that land, next to the railroad tracks, was called Ontario, and the field

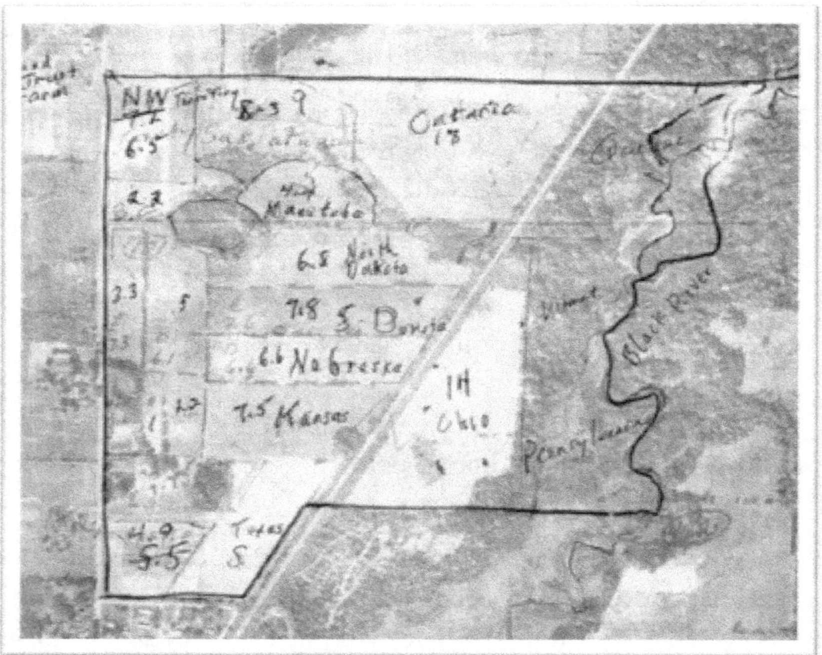

The fields of the farm

along the road in the northwest corner was called Northwest Territory. In between was a pasture we called Manitoba and a few smaller tracts, such as wetlands and woodlands, which never got any names.

The addition of this land to the farm reinforced my plan to develop a dairy enterprise to replace the income that would be lost if and when I retired from teaching. This did happen at the end of 1986 and by then we had had an income from milk since 1980. Sally was very reluctant about the dairy enterprise, and I was soon tired of it too, especially during the months when I had to teach courses in the winter semester after getting up early to milk cows. I also found the smell of cowshit on my clothes to be increasingly disagreeable. But I stayed with it until about

Adrian and me on the tractor near the maple house

1986, when I got my stepson Jon Towne to do most of the milking. For two or three years prior to 1980 I had the Holstein cows bred by artificial insemination, and it did improve the cows thus added to the herd. And then, when the end of the dairy decade (1980 to 1990) was imminent, I bought an Angus bull in 1987 to begin the transformation of the herd back to beef.

The increased income from selling milk, plus the early retirement incentive payment and unused sick leave from WMU, enabled us to finally buy the farm equipment we needed to keep pace with a larger farm operation. In 1984 I bought an unused Deutz 6507 tractor with front wheel assist that had been on dealers' lots for some years, unsold and at a reduced price because of the farm crisis. It also included a very useful front end loader with two buckets. At that time I also purchased a four-bottom moldboard plow, a large chisel plow, a culti-mulcher, a Deutz disc hay mower, a Deutz hay conditioner, and other tillage tools. At last I felt like a real farmer on a real farm. And I enjoyed the more relaxed work of a beef farmer until we needed to sell parts of the farm in 2002.

Of our 160 plus acres, about 90 acres were usually in cropland with another 20 in permanent pasture. About 6 acres were devoted to buildings, gardens and orchards and the remainder was woods and wetlands. One advantage of living on a farm is that several garden plots can be developed on various soils in various parts of the farmstead. This makes crop rotation easier and allows the grower to match different crops to different soils that suit them best. The possibility of various soils was enhanced after 1976 when we hired a man with an enormous crane to dig out the shallow pond behind the barn. The muck he dredged out of that mudhole, enriched by years of livestock standing in the water, was spread out after it dried and made excellent garden soil. After two or three plots were developed around the pond we finally had eleven plots of different soils. We also planted an orchard on the side of the hill near the pond and a vineyard nearby.

Since Bangor is only ten miles from Lake Michigan, we enjoyed the advantages of living close to the Lake. Because that massive body of water changes temperature slower than land, we have cooler springs which help to retard blooming of fruit trees and thus reduces the likelihood of damage by frost. And, of course, fall temperatures remain moderate for a longer time. So we are part of the lake shore fruit belt, surrounded by orchards, vineyards, and blueberry plantations, with a few small diversified farms remaining. In fact, Michigan is said to be second, after

California, in the diversity of its agricultural produce. We probably could have raised more fruit as a profitable crop, but, although it is possible, we held off because it is difficult to do without chemical pesticides on an organic farm.

The practice of rotating crops is even more important on larger fields, and we maintained a system of crop rotation. It began by plowing an old hay field in which very

Cleaning the muck out of the pond

little alfalfa, the choice crop for hay, was growing. Before the field was plowed, cow manure, which we stored in a special manure shed, was spread and plowed in the same day to conserve the volatile ammonia for fertilizer. Then the corn was planted, cultivated two or three times and harvested in fall. The corn stalks were disced down, either in fall to seed winter wheat or in the following spring to seed oats. Either of these worked well as nurse crops to help the very small and fragile alfalfa plants get started. Once the hay crop was started it continued to produce two or three cuttings each year for four or five years until the alfalfa was crowded out by grasses, after which it might be

pastured for another year or two before the cycle of crop rotation started again. Since tillage was only necessary in this system for a year or two out of six or seven years, it was seen as a soil conserving process which caused minimal soil erosion.

As a result of this cropping pattern, and perhaps also because I was known as an organic farmer, I was honored as the "Conservation Farmer of the Year" in 1983 in Van Buren County. This would have been a simple matter of accepting a certificate at a dinner and thanking the Soil Conservation Board. But in 1983 Van Buren County was also honored as the Conservation County of the year in Michigan because it maintained a tree nursery to provide trees for planting. So it happened, synchronously, that a representative of the Soil Conservation Board and I were given a free trip to Phoenix, Arizona, paid for by the Goodyear Tire Company. Not only were farmers from every state in the union lavishly wined and dined, we were bedded in king-sized beds, a first for me. And during the days we were given tours all around Phoenix with lectures on conservation topics.

I remember how farmers from different regions of the country reflected regional characteristics. The paunchy corn-fed farmers from the corn belt were overweight, probably from lack of exercise as they drove tractors. The ranchers from the Southwest were lean and tough, as were the vegetable growers from the New England states. There were a few female farmers and some farm wives. Although

I would have had to pay the air fare, I really should have taken Sally with me. The award was made out to "Maynard and Sally Kaufman."

An unexpected bonus of this award was that I received a hand-written congratulatory note from my doctoral dissertation adviser, Professor Nathan Scott. He had read and approved my doctoral dissertation entitled "James Joyce and the Temptation of Modern Gnosticism." Because I sometimes assumed that the distance between the University of Chicago and my farm was too far to be bridged, this was a great surprise to me. It was also quite a stretch for me, after six years in graduate school, to go back to the farm when I started a teaching career. So our topic has been, and remains, "From James Joyce to Organic Farming." I did not think much about farming when I was a graduate student in Chicago, but as soon as I left the city I was obsessed with farming.

Nearly all the fields on the farm were separated by woody hedgerows overgrown with a variety of trees. Although this used some land and took moisture from the crops during dry periods, I valued the hedge rows for their ecological function. They attracted birds which helped to control insect pests. Over the years I added trees along fences where there were none.

Although there was one field beyond the railroad tracks, mostly within the original 80 acres, beyond that was woodland. About two thirds of the woodland was on higher ground and consisted mainly of sugar maple and red oak. Then, going down toward the river there were wetlands with other varieties of trees and shrubs. One of the main species there was white ash, and most of these trees have died or are dying due to infestations of the emerald ash borer. The trees have generally been a tremendous resource on the farm, yielding fence posts, firewood, lumber for building projects on the farm or for cash sale, along with maple syrup. Since they needed no investment for planting, as annual crops did, their net income per acre was probably as much as farmland.

Another set of historical circumstances may contribute to an understanding of the beginning of this farm. The area around Bangor was a densely wooded ancient forest. The trees were so abundant, even as late as the 1870s, that investors were encouraged to set up a blast furnace in Bangor. This created a need for charcoal which required firewood at the rate of 125 cords daily and cleared the woods at a rate of one square mile per year. Long before this, however, sawmills were operating since 1842 with power from the Black River. The big sawmill operator was Joseph Nyman, who was said to produce 12,000 board feet of lumber per day during the 1860s through the 1880s. Trees had to be cut to produce this lumber and charcoal for the blast furnace. Thus forests were cleared and farming was made possible. A. J. Hull could have been farming and building barns in the 1870s. His farm was only a mile or two from Bangor.

But even the woodland that remained included an incredible variety of species of trees. Once I had learned to identify all the trees, I found that we had at least 75 different species. Over the years I added a few more and a variety of fruit trees. As I studied the qualities and uses of different trees, I gradually learned which trees were best suited to which uses. Fence posts, for example, must be durable in contact with the ground. Mulberry and sassafras are good; black locust is even better and I planted a few in sandy ground where they could spread. As one who grew up in the prairie state of South Dakota with very few native species of trees, I developed a great appreciation for the trees in Michigan. Our apprentices also loved walking in the woods, as did visitors to the farm, so it served a recreational function as well as a source of income.

We began tapping our sugar maple trees as soon as we moved on the farm and enjoyed the maple syrup. Although we began by tapping just a few trees for our own use, we gradually expanded the number of trees we tapped so that there was a surplus for sale. We hung a sign along the road, advertising that we had maple syrup for sale. Soon we were visited by the maple syrup inspector who warned us that if we advertised and sold syrup without inspection we would be shut down and fined. So we enlisted his help in advising us how to build a maple house and what kind of equipment was needed. Once we complied with his recommendations he approved our system and we could legally sell syrup. Eventually, after we rented trees from our neighbor to the north, we were tapping about 525 taps into 135 of our trees and about 100 of our neighbor's. By this time the sale of maple syrup was adding a sizable share to the farm's income.

Gathering and boiling sap to make maple syrup

Although tapping trees was hard work, which required drilling holes into trees with a brace and 7/16 inch bit and tapping the spiles into the holes, along with carrying pails of sap, we enjoyed making maple syrup more than other kinds of farm work. This may be because it was the first outdoor activity after winter and initiated us into spring. It also involved the whole family. Boiling the sap down to syrup was tedious, but was often made enjoyable by the fact people came out to help with tapping or to buy syrup and visit as we boiled the sap. We also soon learned to advertise our season for apprentices to start on the first of February so they could experience the maple syrup operation. We and our students also enjoyed learning about it in Helen and Scott Nearing's very useful *Maple Sugar Book.*

Along with harvesting maple syrup, we also enjoyed what we could harvest from the many fruit trees that were already growing on the farm. Although we planted more fruit trees, they took years to bear fruit. Since apples were grown on some of the fields years ago, there were many seedlings of apple growing in the hedge rows, and a few were good for eating out of hand. We also picked a lot of them and had them pressed into a tart cider by a neighbor who had a large cider press.

Looking back on my farming now, I think I could have done better. As I learned about permaculture, for example, I realized that tree crops might have provided an income comparable to what the farm made with a lot less ecological disruption. My stepson Jon Towne promoted permaculture on the neighboring Land Trust farm and hosted one of the first Permaculture Design courses in Michigan there in 1985, so I learned about it but failed to practice it. While the tillage I did was minimal, it was not harmless. Our traditional grains, such as corn, wheat, or oats, are annual grasses that put their energy into producing seed, but their roots are barely big enough to make the plant grow unless competing weeds are removed. This is done by cultivation in cornfields, which leaves the soil loose and subject to erosion. Because they focus on producing seed, annual grains have provided abundant food so that the human population could grow, but they are destroying the soil on which these crops could continue to grow. Thus, as J.

Russell Smith argued in his book of 1929, *Tree Crops*, "corn, the killer of continents, is one of the worst enemies of the human future." I have come to see corn as a four-letter word. Much too much is planted in our area now.

The alternative to annual grasses such as corn is perennial grains, such as are being developed at the Land Institute, or tree crops, perennials with deep roots that can live through droughts or violent rainstorms which would otherwise increase erosion. Trees can slow the process of climate change as they sequester more carbon in the soil, and they need less tillage so that less carbon dioxide is emitted by oxidation. Tree crops can increase the area of cropland as they are planted on hilly land not suited for annual crops. By leafing out earlier and holding leaves later, they extend the growing season. Tree crops are compatible with traditional livestock which can be fenced in to consume the various products of different trees in season. And the fruits and nuts of trees can be eaten by humans as well as livestock. Even more important, trees are native to this area and should be returned to it.

Selling Parts of the Farm

As Barbara and I began thinking about retirement and planning for it, I remember that I was reluctantly acquiescent. I felt I would rather continue the life I so enjoyed. But in fact we worked on planning for retirement together. For a while we looked for land and a place to live in other areas. The area west of Three Rivers was an attractive possibility and we went there frequently in the summer of 1999 or earlier. Eventually Barbara, who enjoyed walking her dog, Suki, over the fields here near Bangor, said, in effect, "these fields are so beautiful, why don't we build a house on our land and sell the old farm house and buildings." So, in about 2000, that is what we began to do. I was, after all, 71 years old by then.

Since I had already been through the wrenching experience of selling a place which I worked so hard to "improve," (the place on M Avenue) selling was not as difficult as it might otherwise have been. And since we met, through accidental contacts, with a young organic grower, Dennis Wilcox, who wanted to buy the land beyond the railroad, it was only that marginal and distant land that we began selling. In summer of 2002 Dennis bought about 28 acres east of the railroad. In 2015 he sold it to Erin Swystun and Christopher Passmore. They worked together for about a year, but after serious disagreements, she left him. He is doing a good job of raising vegetables organically and selling them on the wholesale market.

Meanwhile, during this time we were planning for our new house and hired Thom Phillips to build it. He had been a student of mine at WMU and served as an instructor on the Land Trust Homesteading Farm. Then he began a career building upscale houses, but felt some dissatisfaction about wasting lumber. So he was available to plan and build for us.

The off-grid house we built in 2001

We situated the house on a sandy hill on the west end of Field 6.8, North Dakota, and in view of a marshy area that soon became a pond after I found a man with the needed digging equipment. We understood that if we were to sell the big brick house and out-buildings we would need to have another place to live. After we moved to this new off-grid house with renewable energy in 2001, we began to advertise the rest of the farm. A notice in the newsletter of Michigan Organic Food and Farm Alliance brought three inquiries. The one from Lee and Laurie Arboreal resulted in the sale of the buildings and about 40 acres to them in 2003. They raised vegetables with organic methods for both wholesale and retail markets and maintained a Community Supported Agriculture arrangement. Eventually Lee left and Laurie took over management of the farm, and is doing an excellent job of it.

In order to vacate the farm so it would be ready for Lee and Laurie, we had to schedule an auction sale. I loved auction sales in my earlier years here in Bangor, and bought many farm tools and supplies at auctions on the assumption that I would eventually be able to sell them at my auction sale. I had done a lot of psychological preparation for this event, recognizing that I would eventually die and would no longer be farming. So the auction in 2003 became a spiritual discipline of letting go. As a result I sold a lot of things that I subsequently had cause to regret, such as a surveyors transit that I got from my father-in-law, Herb Wright, or an 8-foot crowbar that was on the farm, and my great collection of homesteading books. And the irony was that the prices we got at the sale were quite low with only a few "antique" items getting a good price. As it turned out the auction sale was by no means the end of my life, and I have often wished for the things I so willingly put up for sale.

Finally, late in 2008, we sold 44.46 of the 60 acres west of the railroad to Ron and Suzanne Klein. This land included the best and most productive land we had, and I am glad to see that they have used it only to graze a herd of dairy goats. It is probably sequestering more carbon. The land sold to the Kleins was to have been the first part of our proposed "Solar-Reliant Ecovillage." Conditions were not propitious for an ecovillage during the housing collapse of 2008. Selling land provided us with money to live on once the farm income was gone.

Now all we have left of the 160 acres is about 27 acres of good farmland around the new house and about the same number of acres, more or less, in woods and wetland between the railroad and the river. We have considered putting the woods into a conservation easement, but that is a very costly way of making the land worth less. I still have some farm equipment, including the no longer new Deutz tractor, and it is useful for cutting and hauling firewood. But since I have enough dead trees where I live, I no longer go across the railroad tracks to harvest firewood.

Chapter III: The Deep Roots of my Environmentalism

I don't recall that I was aware of environmental issues when I was in college or graduate school. But I do recall that I was increasingly starved for contact with nature, especially when living in Chicago. I would take long walks or bicycle rides in the parks on either end of the Midway Plaisance that runs past the south side of the University Quadrangle. I also managed to get a couple of small part-time jobs caring for lawns. That reintroduced me to a kind of outdoor work and helped to keep me going until we would be able to leave Chicago.

Bicycling with son Karl on Midway Plaisance

I have already reviewed the haste with which we looked for and found a farm to buy in only a few months after moving from Chicago to Kalamazoo. And I was very enthusiastic about getting that run-down farm into production. It was probably through farm activities that I began to feel like an environmentalist and be recognized as an environmentalist on campus. Of course the environment was becoming a hot topic during this time and I probably internalized those cultural concerns. In early spring of 1970, the year of Earth Day, I was teaching at Western and attended a meeting or two, along with three of my colleagues in Religion, in which possible environmental programs on campus were discussed. Because I spoke up about the need for an environmental curriculum, I assume, I was appointed to the university-wide Committee on Environmental Programs. There I worked specifically with a sub-committee whose task it was to design the curriculum. Later, just before I started my half-time leave of absence from classroom teaching, I was elected to chair the Committee On Environmental Programs and did so for a few months.

Also at about this time I was asked to be the convener of a discussion group on the Physical Environment at the annual "Week of Work" (annual conference) for Kent Fellows. Since I had recently met Paul Shepard who was writing books on environmental topics, I invited him as the "expert" and he accepted and gave us interesting ecological tours in the Santa Cruz region. I was certainly not academically prepared in that field and had never taken a course in biology, or ecology, in my life, though I had been reading informally in that area and did so for quite some time. Despite this formal ignorance, however, these environmental activities led me to think of myself as qualified to "teach" in the School of Homesteading that we were proposing. What I was proposing here was a more ecological approach to raising food as opposed to the industrial mode of production, but it broadened into an ecological critique. I also began to offer a regular course in Religion and Environmental Studies called "Religion and Ecological Awareness."

Environmental concerns that were more generalized did motivate other activities later in my life. When I retired from teaching the first public thing I did was to initiate what I called a Green Politics Reading Group. I had begun talking about green politics on campus in connection with the writing I was doing on a projected book called "Visions of a New Earth: Apocalypse and the Transformation of Utopia." My public talk in 1985 was called

State-wide Green meeting on our farm at summer solstice, 1988

"Visions of a New Earth: The Possibility of Green Politics." But the reading group did not start meeting until 1987 because the organizing was postponed until Mona Moormann could attend. She volunteered to publish a newsletter for the group, Southwestern Michigan Greens, and she did so until spring of 1994. We were probably the first Green group to organize in Michigan, although Green groups emerged later in 1987 in Ann Arbor and in East Lansing. Sally and I hosted a state-wide Green meeting on our farm in 1988 which included a summer solstice ritual. And at this time our local group included about 50 regular members, including several of my colleagues from Environmental Studies. They argued for and organized recycling programs but I wrote a little article which suggested that when a calf on the farm had diarrhea we worried more about what went in at the front end than what came out at the back end.

Another leader in the group was a young man, Eric Nelson. He and I attended the first national Green conference in Amherst, Massachusetts, where I led about three discussion groups. It was my first introduction to the Greens as a national political movement. We also attended the national Green conference in Eugene, Oregon. On our way home we missed our flight in Chicago and, since neither of us had a credit card, we had to spend the night at the O'Hare airport. Sally and I also attended the first meeting of the Michigan Green Party in 1989 (even though she was already quite sick and died the next year). Later Barbara and I attended national Green gatherings in West Virginia and in Minneapolis.

This Green Politics activity during the 1980s was the first of three different activities in Green movements. The second was a Van Buren County Greens group in which Barbara and I were active from 2004 to 2008. When the leader of the group, Chuck Jordan, confessed that he was burned out, we transformed the group, with full cooperation of active members, to a chapter of the Transition organization founded by Rob Hopkins in England. The subtitle of his book, *The Transition Handbook*, explains the purpose of the transition movement: *From oil dependency to local resilience.* We, Transition Van Buren-Allegan, were the 49th Transition group in this country. This was a so-called "hub" and some of the local groups we started continued for several more years.

My third participation in Green Politics was once again on the national level. In 2007 Linda Cree, a Green leader from upper Michigan, asked me to represent Rural Greens at the Green Convention in Chicago. I considered it an honor and prepared a talk on "Agrarian Revival at the End of Cheap Oil." This topic was what I was working on at that time as I wrote my book, *Adapting to the End of Oil: Toward An Earth-Centered Spirituality.* The talk I gave was later revised for publication in *Green Horizons*, the national Green magazine edited by John Rensenbrink, the main Green leader in this country. In the next few years he published at least six more of my articles on ecological topics.

My book of 2008, *Adapting to the End of Oil*, is clearly another manifestation of my environmental orientation. As a former Religion Professor I felt the need for a more ecological religious orientation, so I dealt with that under the subtitle of the book, "*Toward an Earth-Centered Spirituality*," in its second part. The book was based on the "peak oil" idea that was current in the early 21st century, but it generalized that idea to include not just running out of oil, but using so much that the pollution of greenhouse gases, such as carbon dioxide, itself limits what can be burned. The unlimited burning of fossil fuels has and will have disastrous effects as it warms the climate. As people used less oil, and used it more efficiently, and as more was produced by "fracking," the glut that resulted in low prices is giving us the wrong signals about using oil now at the time of intensifying climate change.

A final manifestation of my environmentalism was the house we built when I retired from farming. (The house is pictured on page 54.) Since it is off-grid it needs batteries to store power when the sun does not shine and the wind does not blow. Electricity is generated by a set of 1000 watt photo-voltaic panels, mounted on a tracker that moves to face the sun, and by two wind generators rated at 1000 watts each but with actual output dependent on the strength of the wind. Our house also relies on renewable energy for heat with many south facing windows, hydroponic heating in the concrete floor, and a masonry stove which provides efficient and long-lasting heat by burning wood. The ceramic firebox radiates heat for many hours so that the stove needs to be fired only once a day to keep the house warm. Solar panels on the south side of the house help to heat water, along with a loop that thermosiphons through the masonry stove. We were certainly the first in our neighborhood to install renewable energy and among the handful of early adopters of renewable energy in our county. And our rationale for doing so was to illustrate an alternative to the burning of fossil fuels for home heating and electrical power which cause global warming.

The question to be answered in this chapter is, how did I somehow become an environmentalist? The two main contexts in which to search for an answer include my boyhood on a farm and my graduate education in the Divinity School. A third context will be explored briefly: my cultural heritage as a Mennonite.

Growing Up on a Farm in South Dakota

It was one of life's little ironies that as I grew up on a small farm in the 1930s, when the drought and dust storms kept farms from being very productive, as a boy I had already decided that while growing up on a farm was nice, I was not going to be a farmer. I could not regard it as a dependable way to make a living. So after college I went to graduate school in the Divinity School of the University of Chicago and prepared for a career as a professor in a Religion Department. But the course of my life did make me into a farmer and that undermined my career as a religion professor. This Memoir is an attempt to understand and explain why my life turned out so differently from my intentions.

I was born in 1929 on the small farm where my parents eventually lived for fifty-nine years. Our farm was only 80 acres but sometimes my father would rent another 40 or 80

The farm on which I grew up in South Dakota

acres. When I was growing up we farmed with horses. Only in my late teens did my father buy on old tractor with steel wheels. We used it mostly for plowing, but I remember the much more pleasant experience of plowing with four horses pulling a one-bottom plow on which I was riding. I heard only the snorting of the horses, the creaking of the harness, the tearing of roots in the soil, and the songs of the many birds flying around.

Those of us who lived through the dust storms in the 1930s were fully conscious of the fact that humans were responsible for that ecological disaster by plowing the grasslands of the Great Plains. Periodic droughts were not unusual on the Great Plains, but the many plowed fields made the drought of the 1930s an unprecedented disaster as the soil was literally blown away. Native Americans who watched white men plowing simply commented: “Wrong side up.”

My parents were Mennonites, quite religious, and they took us six children to church at least twice on Sundays. My sisters had piano lessons and a regular family pastime in the evenings was for parents and sisters to gather around the piano and sing hymns. I, the oldest boy, felt uncomfortable about joining them and usually excused myself and went out to “hunt” or walk around. This refusal certainly reinforced a tendency toward rebelliousness in me which led to arguments with my father, often about religion. But I spent an enormous amount of time outdoors, sometimes just walking but often hunting. Pheasants were abundant and I often shot one in season and cleaned it for my mother to cook.

So, even as I tried to distance myself from parts of my religious heritage, I was also distanced from the secular society by my adherence to Mennonite pacifism. During World War Two my parents inculcated a distrust of mainstream media by constantly pointing out that various stories in the newspaper were “war propaganda.” Although they did not separate us from “the world” as radically as our religious relatives, the Amish, my siblings and I were discouraged from much modern technology or media.

We had a pond behind our woods with a stone pile next to it so I could sneak up to the pond and shoot wild ducks. With a 12 gauge shotgun I sometimes shot two or three with one shot when they were clustered. Canada geese also stopped at our pond in their migration, but they were so wary that I never got a shot at them. They have recently evolved to get used to humans, but when I was hunting they were really wild.

In summer I often went fishing in the Turkey Ridge Creek, about four miles from our farm. I rode my bicycle or our Shetland pony, Jackie, or, if taking a sibling along, we rode in the two-wheel rubber-tired cart pulled by the pony.

In fall and winter I really loved trapping fur-bearing animals. Until the dry years were over, in the early 1940s,

The pond where I shot ducks

we had only skunks, weasels and badgers. When the rains came muskrats, mink, and raccoons moved into our area. This return of water-loving animals was an object lesson in ecology. Later I even had a chance to trap beavers but there was an annual limit of six and a special permit had to be attached to each pelt.

Trapping is a much slower and more deliberate process than hunting; it required more forethought and planning. One had to learn the ways of wild animals in order to catch them, and this was done by paying close attention to where they lived and moved. I caught animals by their feet when they stepped into the steel leg-hold trap. I am aware that such traps are now considered cruel and that animal-rights activists have made fur coats questionable. I am not writing to justify trapping but to explain why I was so fascinated by it and how it made me aware of the inner workings of natural systems.

When I left my home community to go to college and graduate school, my trapping days were over. I did eventually get a farm with ponds and streams and even a river with many signs of wild animals, and I told myself that when I retired I would trap again. But I never did and I sold the traps at my auction sale. Nor did I hunt although deer and wild turkey were abundant in my woods and fields. For years I did not even shoot woodchucks, whose prior residence I respected, even though they had a nasty way of making their burrows in alfalfa fields where a load of hay bales would be spilled when the wheels fell into a hole. Eventually I did start shooting woodchucks but only until Barbara got dogs that could kill them more efficiently than I could. Even red foxes, which were plentiful on the farm for many years, did not tempt me, although I did give permission to others to trap them.

But I did go back to wild animals in my dreams. For years I had recurring dreams of entering into the burrows of wild animals. The opening was like a well-used woodchuck or badger hole. Although I was usually anxious and full of trepidation, I would somehow crawl in; I felt compelled to crawl in to see how it was. As I went down, the burrow got larger and gradually opened into a well-lit chamber. Different animals were present and sometimes they would offer to show me their "digs" in a most hospitable manner, as if they were honored by my visit. But in many other dreams I encountered a sort of tribunal, usually with a wolf or several wolves presiding on a raised dais. They were not hostile but they were very serious. They did not speak, but looked at me expectantly; and often, in my dream, I would break out into nervous explanations of why I was there.

As a boy constantly wandering over fields and meadows, "hunting," I felt what I would later recognize as numinousity, a sense of the sacred. And I also recognized this as that which William Wordsworth felt as the spiritual presence in nature. This was given by the total immersion I experienced in nature. It was this kind of experience that provided grounding for my eventual environmental concerns and may have lent an ethical urgency to my environmentalism.

The Influence of Process Philosophy in the Divinity School

The influence of process philosophy should be understood only in the most generalized manner, as a kind of intellectual atmosphere rather than any explicit party line. Much of the Whiteheadian influence in the Divinity School was the result of Bernard Loomer's general promotion of process thought in theology in preceding years. I was a student there from 1957 to 1963, just after Loomer's term as dean ended, so I got a full measure of process influence. The main philosopher who is identified with process thinking is Alfred North Whitehead, who published his culminating work, *Process and Reality*, in 1929. I read much of this book in a course on Whitehead taught by Professor Loomer in my final year in the Divinity School. But it is a difficult book and I sat in on the course as an auditor and not for credit, so there was much I did not understand even though I absorbed some general ideas. (The discipline of writing a paper in a course is necessary if one is to fully enter into the subject matter.)

Whitehead called his system a philosophy of organism, in which feeling is primary—both physical and conceptual feelings. He disagreed with "substance" thinkers and argued that "how an actual entity becomes constitutes what that actual entity is." The principle of process is that the 'being' of an actual entity is constituted by its 'becoming'. This surely makes sense, but because the language of substance philosophy evolved with nouns and verbs it distorts the principle of process. Thus Whitehead had to invent a new technical terminology which makes his writing difficult to read. Actual entities, or actual occasions, do not stand alone; they are real only to the extent that they are in relationship.

The emphasis on relationship was carried on by Charles Hartshorne in books such as *Reality as Social Process* and *The Divine Relativity*. His books helped me to understand that a God who is absolute is absolved from relationship and essentially irrelevant. Hartshorne did not identify himself as a theologian, but thought about God as a philosopher of religion in the Department of Philosophy at the University of Chicago.

The focus on God was central in the thought of both Whitehead and Hartshorne. Whitehead emphasized the dipolar nature of God, as both primordial and consequent. In the consequent nature God is affected by, or suffers, what happens in the world. This aspect of God is fully relative. It is here that process thinking provides the basis for an environmental ethic to those who understand this relationship between God and the world. It certainly contributed to my respect for ecological integrity.

Hartshorne also developed the idea of panentheism, which affirms both the transcendent nature of God, as in classical theism, and the immanent becoming of God, as in pantheism. Thus the world is in God, but God is also more than the world. This is illustrated in the analogy of organism, which sees the world as the body of God while God is the mind that cares for us—cells, as it were, in the divine body. These ideas about God, incidentally, are paradigmatic, since God, in process thinking, is not an exceptional case, but the ultimate exemplar of relationships in the world. Thus the process view of the world is permeated with references to God.

By the time I was in my final year in the Divinity School and worked out my own theological position, my

"Manifesto," I spent over a page out of five pages explaining how important process thinking was to me. I argued that it makes possible the transition to a post-Christian epoch which would see the Holy Spirit (creativity) rather than Jesus Christ (salvation) as the dominant aspect of the Trinity.

My understanding of how process thinking led to environmentalism was greatly helped by an article written by Ron Engel. He had come through the Divinity School and had written a book, *Sacred Sands*, which was focused on the dunes along the south end of Lake Michigan and their preservation from industrial expansion. Engel's article, "Making the Earth Covenant at Chicago," reviews the prevalence of process thinkers in the Divinity School and lists those who were most influential, starting in the late 1940s. And as he moves into the 1960s, more such thinkers on his list are recognized as environmentalists. He gives credit for this both to evolutionary thinking and to the influence of a process orientation. And he recognizes that the environmental emphasis was reinforced in many of these scholars by how and where they chose to live, with summer homes in places like the Lake Michigan Dunes. And some who graduated from the Divinity School, such as John Cobb, have become leaders of Christian environmentalism in books such as *Is it Too Late?* and *A*

Swift Hall, the home of the Divinity School

Christian Natural Theology. Coming just after a time when we were taught that God acts in history, the re-emergence of natural theology, now based on Whitehead, was a great achievement. In one of his books Cobb has a chapter entitled "Whitehead: An Ecological Philosophy."

My major professor, Preston Roberts, was not mentioned in Engel's article of 2008. By this time Preston had already suffered a nervous breakdown. But shortly before this he wrote "A Theology for Christian Critics" as a kind of guideline. In it he discusses the importance of process philosophy which he recognizes as the second most important influence on his thinking, second only to his Quaker background. He had been a student of Loomer's and was retained on the faculty of the Divinity School to start the Religion and Art program in 1948. In this article he shows how process thinking is helpful even in the art of literary analysis, interpretation and evaluation.

I have reviewed the influences that shaped my environmental concerns. The rural influence very likely helped me move toward the homesteading ideal. Later I gradually came to recognize the importance of sustainable and organic agriculture. Too often urban environmentalists fail to recognize the importance of food at all, not to mention ecological agriculture. I have published articles that call attention to this omission.

The influence of process philosophy shaped my more comprehensive worldview along ecological lines so that now the threat of climate change looms ominously in my mind and has for the past quarter century. This issue has become more serious since Donald Trump was elected president and denied the seriousness of climate change. His policies could retard the mitigation of climate change, and the unfortunate reality is that many citizens seem to agree with his denial. Or they do not believe it is possible to give up our industrial way of life now still powered by fossil fuels.

My Cultural Heritage as a Mennonite

Mostly by unconscious assimilation I absorbed some aspects of my cultural history as an Anabaptist-Mennonite. My ancestors on my father's side, who were known as the Swiss Brethren led by Conrad Grebel in 1523, left Switzerland later in the sixteenth century after getting into trouble with authorities because they rejected infant baptism and insisted on adult baptism. My mother's people left the Netherlands for the same reason at about the same time. Thus they became Anabaptists, rebaptised, and they were called Mennonites after Menno Simons, their Dutch leader.

During the seventeenth and eighteenth centuries these Anabaptist-Mennonites wandered over Europe, often persecuted because they questioned the validity of the Christianity of more conventional Christians. As they wandered they sometimes found land for farming on the estates of wealthy noblemen. Here they soon became known as expert farmers, and in C. Henry Smith's history of the Mennonites, we learn that a Mennonite farmer "introduced the principle of rotation of crops on his farm, and use of clovers in place of fallowing, selective stock breeding, and other improved methods of agriculture now everywhere practiced." Later, in 1763, The Russian Empress, Catherine II, herself of German descent, invited Mennonites and other Germans to settle on Russian lands in the Ukraine. Here they were expected to serve the Russian peasantry as an exemplary model in the pioneering and cultivation of lands newly acquired from the Turks. These German immigrants were granted religious freedom, and, of special value to pacifistic Mennonites, exemption from military service.

According to Karl Stumpp in his history of the German Russians, the privileges granted to Mennonites and other German-speaking people in Russia ended in 1871 when Alexander III instituted an anti-German policy that ended the exemption from military service for Germans. In a few years, mostly in 1874-1875, my ancestors then again emigrated, this time to the Great Plains of the Dakotas and Kansas where they settled as pioneer farmers. One of those who came with the new settlers was my great grandfather Christian Kaufman who, according to his obituary, was said to be *Ammisch-erzogen*, raised by the Amish. Some Mennonites were Amish in the old country and left the Amish sect when they came to this country.

Throughout their European history, Mennonites were a rural people recognized as resourceful and careful farmers. The Amish have more faithfully maintained their cultural cohesiveness even after they settled in this country. Perhaps they were more careful in their choices of agricultural technology and avoided technology that disrupted interdependence within the community. Mennonite farmers were more acculturated to industrial agriculture and, as they adopted more labor-saving technology, Mennonite communities were soon diminished as more and more young people left for urban jobs. Obviously I was one of those who left.

My brother Roy, who has been a pastor in four rural Mennonite congregations, published a book recently in which he argues for the continuation of agrarian life now in a time when far fewer Mennonite farmers remain in our home community, as machines have replaced people on the farm. Most Mennonites today are urban dwellers, and while Roy understands that reduced fossil fuels in the near future will curtail industrial agriculture and open opportunities for more small-scale farming, he makes his argument for more Mennonite farmers on religious grounds. I feel such strong sympathy for his agrarian position as a

Mennonite that, despite my disavowal of its religious or doctrinal aspects as a post-Christian, I have to feel that I remain an ethnic Mennonite and have at least maintained its moral concerns. This adds a dimension of depth to my environmental-agrarian commitment.

Chapter IV: A Doctoral Dissertation on James Joyce

After graduating from Bethel College in North Newton, Kansas, in spring of 1957, and after a summer with relatives in South Dakota, my wife Marian and I headed to Chicago for graduate school. She was planning to study for a Master's degree in the English Department and I enrolled for a Master's Degree in the Divinity School. I went there because an uncle of mine had gone to Chicago years ago to study German, and because my philosophy professor at Bethel recommended the Divinity School. I also favored Chicago because Robert Maynard Hutchins had abolished intercollegiate athletics there and I respected his emphasis on intellectual inquiry. Having majored in English and Philosophy in college, I chose to study in a program called Religion and Art which was focused on Religion and Imaginative Literature. Since I did well in it, I got the Master's degree, and went on for a Ph.D. degree which took several years.

Marian and I drove to Chicago in late summer of 1957 pulling a two-wheel trailer mostly filled with books. We found our way to 47th Street on the south side and lived for the first year in a Black neighborhood at Woodlawn and 47th Street. The Mennonite Biblical Seminary was in that area at the time and we rented an apartment in a building it owned. Seminary students and other graduate students in the Chicago area also lived there and we made friends with a few and I participated in a Mennonite Graduate Group for several years. During the first year or two we explored some of Chicago's points of interest, but mostly we studied. We were especially pleased with WFMT Fine Arts radio and listened to many programs. By the time we started our second year in Chicago the Seminary was moved to Elkhart, Indiana, and we moved to a University-owned apartment at 1164 East 64th Street.

I had a good start in the Divinity School because I came with a Woodrow Wilson Fellowship. This also provided us with enough money so that Marian could take courses in the English Department. This Fellowship was really a lucky break. I had applied with great care, especially in writing the required essay on intellectual development. My interviewer was quite impressed that a farm boy from South Dakota had been reading Partisan Review. When the fellowships were originally announced and I received a list of fellows elected, I read through the list again and again and could not find my name. I was bitterly disappointed. But a few weeks later the Woodrow Wilson Foundation apparently received more funds, gave out more fellowships and I was included on that list. This recognition helped me a great deal in the Divinity School. For my second year there I received a Divinity School scholarship and for my third year a Divinity School Fellowship which included a stipend for living expenses.

My status among students evolved in smaller and more subtle ways. Early on, at the first gathering for students in the Religion and Literature Field, at Nathan Scott's house one evening, somebody quoted someone who said, "I shot an arrow in the air, and where it flew I know not where." After a pause I responded: "What goes up must come down." This was followed by a buzz of comments in respectful tones: "cyclical return" "erotic realism" and other comments. I realized I should ride on this response and say no more that evening. Because I found my fellow students exceptionally intelligent and interesting, I finally learned to be more outgoing and popular. In college I was a married and very bookish student. I also made friends with students in the fields of Constructive Theology and History of Religions. Many of us in the field of Religion and Literature were snobs and looked down on those in more pedestrian disciplines such as Bible or Church history. We felt we were redefining sacred literature.

I also made friends when I worked in the Swift Hall Coffee Shop, "where God drinks coffee," according to the cup that Barbara brought back from there a few years ago. During the years I was there the Divinity School was mainly a graduate school in Religion. In contrast to its roughly 300 students in Masters and Doctors programs, only about six were in the Bachelor of Divinity program for students planning to enter into the ministry. During the years I was in the Divinity School, the Christian ministry had very little prestige.

Swift Hall and Bond Chapel connected by a Cloister

Most of all I was helped by Preston Roberts, the founder and Chair of the Field of Religion and Art. In my first course with him, in my first quarter in the Divinity School, I wrote a paper called "A Christian Theory of Literature with Reference to Joyce's Portrait." Pres apparently liked the paper very much. In his comments on the paper, handed out a few months later, he wrote as follows:

> This is by far the best of the papers I received this year. In fact it is as good as any paper it has been my privilege to read for as long as I can remember. Moreover, I have learned more about Joyce from reading it than from any other critical essay I have

> come across to date. What more can I say? Unless to thank you for it and to confess that I have been inspired and humbled by it.

I was then asked to read this paper to a Religion and Literature colloquium and it was subsequently published in *Quest, a Journal of Student Opinion.* As I re-read the paper recently, after many years, I thought it could have been better, and the version that I used in my dissertation was indeed much better.

Another paper I wrote that quarter, for John Hayward, generated a comment from him that "this paper is one of the best ever turned in to me." The paper was on "Myth, Theology and Religious Belief."

Aside from teaching me how to make a martini in the townhouse where he and Eileen and their children lived, Pres Roberts, raised a Quaker, educated at Harvard and Chicago where he was retained to start the field of Religion and Art, was my strongest supporter and finally my adviser in my doctoral work. But he found it very difficult to write, although he did write a very wise article laying out a typology for the interpretation of tragedy as a literary-dramatic form in Greek, Christian and Modern contexts and a few other articles. He chose me as his assistant for the year of 1959-1960, and I spent many hours with him, preparing and grading exams and occasionally leading discussions in his introductory courses. But his strength in personal relationships was his professional weakness, a distraction from research and writing.

Since I was a bit competitive as a student in relation to Pres, I argued that his typology of Greek, Christian and Modern should include a Romantic or Gnostic type too. I had done that in relation to *A Portrait*, and also wrote a paper on *Romeo and Juliet* to illustrate the Romantic tragedy. Pres did not argue with me about it, probably because he felt secure with his typology. But I was gratified to see, in what was probably the last paper Pres wrote before he died, a statement indicating that he had heard my argument. He wrote that "there may be a fourth great type of tragedy. It is dark Romantic in literary terms, Manichean in philosophical terms, and Gnostic in religious or theological terms." This was in a paper entitled "The Redemption of King Lear." I filed it away when I got it and only recently read it again as I reviewed his papers.

Marital Difficulties

I was succeeding as a scholar even as I was failing in my marriage. Our son Karl was born on September 26, 1958, and this seemed to hold our marriage together for a year or so. I was very busy with my studies, and early in 1959 I registered as a Ph.D. candidate. After serving a year as Treasurer of the Divinity School Association (the main student group), I was elected its President in June of 1960. Such recognition, however, was offset by personal problems as my marriage was failing and I began an affair with Sally. Marian and I had become increasingly estranged at that time, as were Sally and her husband.

But neither of us were ready for divorce and remarriage—yet. So for another year we were in a limbo of indecision and I was distracted from my academic work. My health suffered and I was often sick and so weak that I had difficulty walking the mile and a half to my classes. I spent several months in group therapy sessions and moved out of the apartment Marian and I had shared, then moved back, then out again. I was learning, on an existential level, that an excessive amount of time devoted to academic learning can be disruptive in a marriage.

In January of 1961 I applied for both a Kent and a Rockefeller fellowship. I took great care writing a 17 page statement for the Kent application. I was awarded the Rockefeller in early March, and the Kent Fellowship in

April. I was the first to receive a Kent Fellowship in the Divinity School for several years, though Pres Roberts and Chuck Long were Kent Fellows long before I came on the scene. Only about thirteen Kent Fellowships were awarded nationwide each year. So it was a bit of a consolation, along with the money which totaled over $5,000. In fact the income from fellowships, which totaled over $13,000 in my years at Chicago until then, saved me from a lot of non-academic work.

But much of this came at the worst time in my life, when my guilt and indecision were nearly paralyzing. I had been trying to return to Marian and failing, while Sally was becoming more distant and even hostile. By late summer, when Marian and I were legally divorced, the issues between us were resolved, and since Sally was also divorced by then, she and I were free to marry. We did that on February 6, 1962 in recognition of the fact that we had discovered that we were each born on that day in 1929. We were married by Al Nichols in the apartment he shared with Marge, his wife and Sally's good friend. A couple of friends and Pres and Eileen Roberts were present to witness the ceremony.

My parents, who refused to recognize remarriage after divorce as anything but legalized adultery, were very slow to accept Sally as a daughter-in-law. Since I knew that the church I grew up in would also not accept remarriage, I wrote a letter to my pastor and resigned my membership. My pastor made a trip to Chicago, not merely to ask me to reconsider, but to remind me that this was a decision that the congregation and I had to make together. I was ready resign in any case for religious reasons, as I was moving into a post-Christian space, so the remarriage was a convenient excuse to do so. As for my parents, I am glad to report that parental love triumphed over theological legalism and, after several years, they accepted Sally and our children.

Meanwhile, I was still trying, and sometimes failing, because of emotional trauma, to be a student. When I was there, candidates for the doctoral degree in the Divinity School were required to pass "Qualifying" or "Comprehensive" exams in eight different fields: Bible (including both Hebrew and Christian scriptures), Church History, History of Christian Thought, Constructive Theology, History of Religions, Religion and Literature, Religion and Personality, and Ethics and Society. Although I had passed some of these exams already, I failed in the two exams I wrote in 1960 and had to take them again. It was customary to take one or two courses in a field as preparation for the exams considered most difficult. I did that and by summer of 1961 I had passed the exams in all eight fields, along with French and German exams. Although this was a theological curriculum, the breadth of inquiry it represented constituted a higher liberal education.

I did get a couple of C grades, one in Church History and one in History of Christian Thought. I simply did not know many historical facts, and to remedy that I constructed a giant historical time chart to gain a better sense for the sweep of world history. The second C was in a course in the History of Christian Thought where I had to take an incomplete because I was bogged down in the morass of marital difficulty. I thought I was on the way to a B, but when I finished the paper and handed it in, the instructor, Jaroslav Pelikan, gave me a C. It could be that the good professor heard about my famous (or infamous) limerick:

"A marvelous bird is the pelican,
His bill can hold more than his belly can,
He can speak for a week
On what's in his beak;
But I don't know how the hell he can."

Passing the Final Exams

A couple of months after we were married Sally and I rented a spacious apartment at 5131 Blackstone, where I enjoyed my final and most fruitful year in Chicago. It was here that I wrote my MA exams in May of 1962 and received an MA degree. Afterwards Pres Roberts invited me over and explained that he had spoken to the dean about the possibility that I might be the third instructor in the Field. The dean, sensitive to questions raised by other faculty members about my divorce and remarriage, could not approve Pres's request. Such questions had also been raised by certain faculty members in 1961 when the faculty considered recommending me for a Rockefeller Fellowship. Since I had been taking a year, six courses, in the English Department in my final year, I was ready to switch to it in case of serious trouble. But other faculty members in the Divinity School, such as Bernard Loomer, took my side and argued that if I was not fit to receive a Fellowship I was not fit to be a student in the Divinity School at all. Apparently nobody was ready to consider expelling me.

Although I was not very anxious about being expelled from the Divinity School, I did also consider switching to the Committee on Social Thought. I was intrigued by the fact that one of its organizers was David Grene, the famous translator of Greek tragedies, who also maintained a small farm south of Chicago. He later wrote a memoir about it entitled *Of Farming & Classics*, in which he praised subsistence farming and even then made me feel nostalgic about it. But I was never serious about leaving the Divinity School and never even bothered to find out where the Committee on Social Thought had its office on the University of Chicago campus.

I completed the written part of my doctoral exam on October 22-25, 1962 and got a grade of A-. I also wrote a paper called "Stephen Dedalus and the Gnostic Heresy in

Aesthetics" which was to be the basis of my oral exam. The oral part of the exam was in early November and it did not go well. Apparently issues about my moral, or immoral, conduct were more interesting than the paper I provided for the discussion. My main adversary was J. Coert Rylaarsdam, who had been the professor in my Old Testament course. His "questions" took the form of accusations and failed to show that he had even read the paper. Norman McLean, from the English Department, clearly did not understand my paper and thought I should have written a different paper. I had taken a course on Wordsworth from him and we seemed to understand each other then. As a mild-mannered and slightly boring English prof he was, incidentally, the last person in the world I might have expected to go back to Montana and write the terrific novel *A River Runs Through It.* But it was a mistake to invite him to my oral exam.

Eventually Rylaarsdam moved that I pass the exam and in so doing precluded the possibility that I pass with distinction. I had been assured by the advisers in my field that the quality of my written exams was pointing to my passing with distinction. I was disappointed, just as I was when I learned that I had been considered as a candidate for a faculty position and rejected. In retrospect, however, I saw that it was a situation fraught with potential problems. It was best that I left Chicago. I had always reported on my marital problems in the most candid manner and in fact I was always accepted and funded as a student in spite of them. That was reassuring

Pseudo-medieval gargoyles on University buildings

to me. And yet I felt then, as I have since, that I failed to realize my potential as a scholar in religion and literature.

Finding a Job

In September of 1961 I was invited, probably through Tom Lawson's intercession, to speak at Kalamazoo College, along with the famous literary critic, Alfred Kazin. The title of my talk was "Christus or Bloom his Name is: the pattern of salvation in Joyce's *Ulysses*." I had already been thinking about the dissertation and the topics I intended to discuss in it. I enjoyed the visit to Kalamazoo and thought it would be nice to teach there, not at Kalamazoo College but at Western Michigan University.

The Kent Fellowship was of extra special value in career-building because in its "Week of Work" (annual conference) programs fellows were brought into close relationship with leading scholars in Religion. I was asked to read my paper on James Joyce at my first Week of Work at Drew University and it was well received by an audience of fellows and established scholars in religion and literature. Eventually these associations did lead to the job I got at Western Michigan University since I met Cornelius Loew at a Week of Work. Cornie, a Kent fellow himself, actually established the Religion Department at WMU with a grant from the National Council on Religion in Higher Education, which also funded the Kent Fellowship program. I had also met Ian Barber, a professor of Physics and Religion at Carlton College in Minnesota, and he invited me to apply there; but since I had been in private schools after grade school, I decided I should try a public university. Late in December of 1962 I went to Kalamazoo to see Cornie again and to interview for a job in his Department of Religion and Philosophy. Cornie said he would try to make a good offer. My starting salary was only $6,500, quite a bit less than the $8,500 I received from fellowships and summer jobs during my last year in Chicago.

I certainly appreciated the financial support my various fellowships provided and the freedom they made possible for study. I did also find jobs: one summer at Montgomery Ward as a guard, another summer in the Post Office, doorman at a nurse's residence, working for families to keep lawns neat, but eventually I swallowed my pride and followed my friend Glen Boese's advice and found jobs as a janitor while regular janitors were on vacation. This job provided big money in a very short time. And it gave me access to the "junk" people were throwing away in their trash.

What I enjoyed most during my years in Chicago were the many discussions and general fellowship with fellow students who shared a common set of interests. Because of this my six years at Chicago were the most rewarding in my academic career, in spite of the anguish of divorce. Unfortunately, I lost track of these fellow-students in a few years. After fifteen years I could claim friendship and regular contact with only one fellow student: Preston Browning. But it was I who dropped out and failed to attend the scholarly conferences and gatherings where colleagues meet.

Harper Memorial Library Reading Room

1963 was my last year in Chicago and the first at Western Michigan University. Our son Conrad was born in January. In February I formally accepted the position in Kalamazoo and we moved there later in summer. In spring of 1963 I offered my parting shot to the Divinity School with my manifesto, "Religious Possibilities in the Post-Christian Epoch." The written version, published in *Quest*, was preceded by an exciting discussion one evening when I read it and two fellow-students read their written responses. Although both critics failed to point out that my notion of the Third Epoch, as based on the Trinitarian view of history espoused by Joachim of Fiore, was a variant of the old Sabellian heresy, both found much to criticize. But this was my major theological statement and it served as a fitting climax to my academic experience. My most rewarding learning experiences occurred in such extra-curricular events.

Pres Roberts and My Dissertation

In 1967 this manifesto, totally revised, was published under the title "Post-Christian Aspects of the Radical Theology" as the final chapter in a book edited by the Death-of-God theologian, Thomas J. J. Altizer, and it stimulated a modest interest among some theologians. It also helped to clarify my theological approach as I was working on my doctoral dissertation, "James Joyce and the Temptation of Modern Gnosticism." But I was distracted from much writing on that by the demands of course preparation as a new instructor and by the run-down farm Sally and I bought very soon after moving to Kalamazoo.

In addition, Pres Roberts suffered a breakdown in February, 1965 which hospitalized him, led to his wife leaving him, and finally to his dismissal from the faculty of the Divinity School. He had been writing only a handful of papers in recent years, and letters to his favorite students, of which I was one. But he could no longer serve as my dissertation adviser. He left Chicago and had therapy in Hartford, Connecticut, ended up teaching a few courses at the College of the Holy Cross in Worcester, MA, and died there in the mid-1970s. It is perhaps fitting that he exemplified so totally in his own life the specifications of modern tragedy as he described it in his theory of tragedy.

Pres had developed a typology of tragedy to show the differences between Greek, Christian and modern types. Each type evolved its own version of the tragic hero, his or her tragic flaw, recognition of what went wrong, and the reversal of the tragic hero's fortune. The modern protagonist suffers some kind of emotional insecurity or anxiety by virtue of which he is unable to take hold of what is possible and is driven to cling to what is impossible. In his essay on "The Redemption of King Lear," written long after his own breakdown, Pres described more of the modern story.

> Their reversal is from bad to worse fortune and from one kind of misery to another. The appropriate emotional reactions to modern tragedy are poignance and despair. We feel poignance because the protagonists are incapable of becoming more than shadows of their former or potential selves. We feel despair because there seems to be no one meaningful way for them to live and so many meaningless ways for them to die. But we also feel a catharsis or mitigation of these emotions because modern protagonists are often able to recognize such pathetic connections between meaninglessness and despair with the harassed, divided, and unfulfilled but stubborn courage of their souls. It is this naked but unflinching recognition of what is pathetic or less than tragic (in the Greek sense) and incapable of redemption (in the Christian sense) in experience which endows modern protagonists with a kind of dignity that is so reminiscent of their Greek and Christian prototypes.

I see this as a kind of "unflinching recognition" by Pres of his own story.

Since Pres Roberts could no longer be my academic adviser and advocate, I appealed to Nathan Scott and he very graciously offered to serve as my dissertation adviser. With his encouragement and guidance I finally finished writing the dissertation. He interceded for me with publishers, but there were no offers to publish another book on Joyce.

Nathan Scott, my teacher and dissertation advisor

As it turned out I had most of the first three chapters of the dissertation pretty well written while I was still in Chicago. These included a fifty-page essay on "Joyce in the View of his Critics," of which the last fifteen specified my understanding of the "Moral and Religious Aspects of Imaginative Literature." The second chapter, even longer, was entitled "The Literary Context: Symbolism and Naturalism," and it explained how symbolism and naturalism informed Joyce's early poems, *Chamber Music,* and his early short stories in *Dubliners.* The third chapter was my third version of how I thought about *A Portrait of the Artist As a Young Man*, now entitled "Stephen Dedalus and the Gnostic Heresy in Aesthetics." These chapters were easier than the four remaining chapters, which included *Exiles*, *Ulysses* and *Finnegans Wake*, and a concluding summary on the changing forms of Joyce's Gnostic tendencies in his career.

Moreover, because of the innovative aspects of Joyce's later works, it is not enough to simply read his works but also, in order to interpret and evaluate them, the enormous library of secondary works of commentary and interpretation they have spawned. This, in addition to the inherent difficulty of *Ulysses* and *Finnegans Wake*, made the dissertation a more demanding task than it seemed when I began. And it took so long that I got sick and tired of it. So after it was finished I put it aside and failed to exploit some very insightful passages for publication. In fact, until I set out to write this chapter I had never once read the whole thing for nearly fifty years. When I did read it through recently I was extremely pleased with it. It is a solid piece of work. But, as I indicated on page 6 above, when I finished the dissertation I was in the midst of writing on a topic much more interesting to me: "The New Homesteading Movement: From Utopia to Eutopia." I was so weary with writing the dissertation that I was able to move enthusiastically into the homesteading movement, not only in that article, but also in reality as I planned my half-time leave of absence from the classroom.

In retrospect, however, the dissertation looks great to me now, and I think it made some original contributions to the interpretation of Joyce. First, of course, is what I called the temptation of modern Gnosticism. Only one doctoral student contacted me who was also exploring that connection, so it seems to be an original approach to Joyce. Gnosticism was a second century heresy in the Christian tradition which argued that the created world was the defective product of an alien and evil God from which, with revealed knowledge, it is possible to escape. It is a dualistic religion of salvation from this world. There are, of course, Gnostic forms of Christianity that are very similar as they too offer salvation from this world. Various forms of Gnosticism have recurred through the centuries, including the Theosophical movement of the 19th century which influenced Joyce through the Symbolist movement.

Two other motifs in Joyce have also found expression in contemporary thinkers. One is the Gnostic imagination with which Joyce was able to destroy and recreate the world in *Finnegans Wake.* I correlated this with Norman Brown's "symbolic consciousness" as articulated in his great work, *Love's Body.* Even Nathan Scott, a Christian critic, asserted that in *Finnegans Wake* Joyce "decided to be God and to create ex nihilo a universe of his own."

The other motif in Joyce's work is the death of God, which I correlated with the radical theology of Thomas J. J. Altizer. Just as Joyce was recognized by some of his most astute critics as an antitheist, so Altizer argued that "only by accepting and even willing the death of God in our lives can we be liberated from a transcendent beyond." In its final two chapters, my dissertation shows how decisive these two motifs are in Joyce's final vision and how Norman Brown and Altizer more recently emerged to reinforce Joyce's final position of modern Gnosticism.

I had chosen the title of this book, *From James Joyce to Organic Farming,* as a juxtaposition designed to call attention to the major shift in my life. But as I finish writing this chapter I see that there may be a hidden connection between James Joyce as a Gnostic writer and organic farming as a way to preserve the earth. While I was fascinated by Joyce's implicit denial of the goodness of the created world as it led him to create a counter-world, I have always believed in the goodness of this created world and it is very likely that I moved into organic farming and organizing to help save the earth from damage done by chemical farming methods. I may not have been fully conscious then of how my concern with Joyce's Gnosticism led me to organic farming.

Chapter V: My Role in the Organic Movement

There are at least a couple of ways of dealing with the way in which homesteading led to the organic movement. The first is on a general cultural level. That is, the new homesteading movement, which grew out of the 1960s, was the result of the back-to-the-land movement and its desire to live in a more ecological manner. As more and more new farmers moved back to the land, the organic movement emerged as a more ecological way to raise food and gradually, in the 1970s, took organized forms of which the movement in Michigan will be described below.

Before we consider local manifestations of this nation-wide trend, there is one other cultural phenomenon we may want to keep in mind. An organization called the National Gardening Association started in 1972 but was especially active in the 1980s, and funded surveys to tabulate the size of gardening activities in this country. Another group, Gardens for All, calculated that home vegetable gardens were grown on 38 million backyards adding up to 1.7 million acres, and estimated the value of that home garden product at 16 billion dollars per year, more than the value of all of California's crops combined. Paul Hawken has argued, in his chapter on "Disintermediation," that "the highly intermediary food business is gradually being dis-intermediated as more people grow their own." He reported that in 1981, according to a Gallup poll, 45 million families had home gardens in which they grew food worth over $14 billion at retail prices, or approximately five percent of the country's total food purchases. In my articles over the years, I pointed out that backyard gardening produced more dollar value, had it been sold, than all the vast cornfields in America. Much of this backyard gardening was done with organic methods.

One other cultural influence at the time was the emphasis on production for use in the household and not just for sale. At the School of Homesteading, with a couple of English majors in the first year, we were avid readers of Wendell Berry's early book of poetry called *Farming: A Hand Book*. Prior to this time I had been reading Berry's more autobiographical book, *The Long-Legged House*. Here Berry was explicitly advocating farming for self-provisioning, a theme he has returned to in his later books. From Berry, more than any other writer, we learned why homesteading is of cultural value. Self-provisioning, according to him, is the taproot of agrarian culture.

On our farm, the transition from homesteading to the organic movement was almost immediate because we did both. Our students arrived in spring of 1973, and it just happened that the first meeting of Organic Growers of Michigan was held in January of that year. We attended these meetings regularly with our students because we felt that it was important for them to recognize the importance of, and participate in, collective action. Needless to say, organic methods of growing were practiced on our farm and I think virtually all our students learned them. This chapter is focused on organic farming and on my efforts in the organic movement. Whatever we did along these lines was done publicly, so that our students could learn from it.

I have to confess that I was a slow starter in the organic movement. On the first farm we bought on M Avenue near Kalamazoo I was showing off some fruit trees I had started in the late 1960s to some students, when the wife of one of them asked why I wanted to spray chemicals. "Why not go organic?" she proposed. That prompt was all I needed and I soon got acquainted with a couple who were among the first organic farmers in the area, Bill and Marie Mundt, near Marcellus, Michigan. They had a field day every summer where people could watch Bill do some chisel plowing. After he stopped and turned off the engine he would sit on his tractor and lecture to the people gathered around, explaining that by tilling in the cover crops, such as buckwheat, he was able to incorporate the cosmic vibrations of solar energy into the soil. It was obvious that it made sense to him, and he raised good crops.

I soon started attending more meetings and conferences, even though there was not yet a formal organization of organic growers in Michigan. At a meeting on a farm near Lansing, Michigan, I heard some old men muttering to each other, "feed the soil, not the plant." After thinking

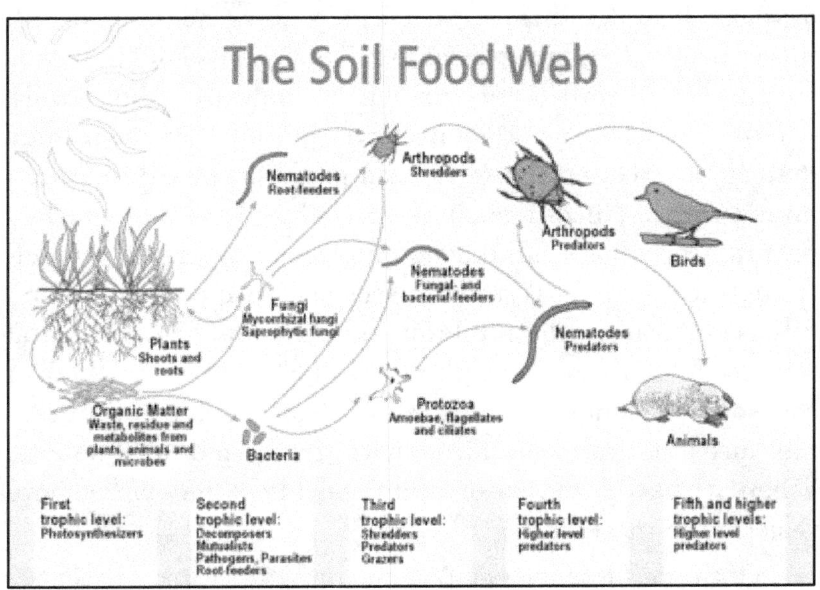

about it, that made a kind of intuitive sense to me. Then, as soil science evolved over the years with researchers such as Elaine R. Ingham, feeding the soil was demonstrated in a more scientific manner. Dr. Ingham is a leader in describing the soil food web. She has been documenting the roles of the various microscopic forms of life in the soil and how they transform organic matter in the soil into nutrients for the growth of plants. As long as forty years ago I could see that organic methods worked, but then I had only the vaguest understanding of how they worked. Those old organic farmers near Lansing should have said "feed the organisms in the soil so they can feed the plant" if they had wanted to give a more comprehensive explanation.

As more was learned about how organic methods worked, there were refinements on those methods. When I was starting out, going "organic" was simply the alternative to chemical fertilizers which had been developed as farms became more specialized and no longer raised livestock to produce manure for fertilizer. After World War II various chemicals, such as surplus nitrates from explosives, were developed for fertilizer, and biocides were adapted to kill insect pests. Organic growers resisted the use of these war surplus materials, not primarily because they were pacifists, but because they preferred natural over synthetic materials. Green manure, compost, barnyard manure, mined rock fertilizers such as rock phosphate and crushed granite, could be used, but no anhydrous ammonia or acid-treated fertilizers. To repel insect pests we purchased and released parasite and predator insects to eat the pests, and we also used less toxic plant-based insecticides. And of course we depended on cultural controls, such as encouraging insect-eating wild birds with trees and bird-houses. When we could we chose plant varieties that were more resistant to insects.

Organic (or biological) and inorganic (or synthetic) systems of growing plants are radically different even though they seem superficially similar. Both work to make plants grow, and the organic system can be of help to the inorganic system. But the converse is not true: the toxic pesticides or high levels of inorganic (synthetic) fertilizers that are often used in inorganic systems can damage the organisms in the soil that feed the plant. In addition, deep tillage in either system can damage the organisms that live in the soil, especially the mycorrhizal fungi that are so important in helping to nourish plants and build soil structure.

The advantages of the organic system are several: It promotes long-term sustainability as it feeds the organisms in the soil with organic matter which those organisms transform into plant food. At the outset, this means that the organic system, which builds humus in the soil, also sequesters carbon, which is 58% of organic matter that is made available as a plant food. The organic system does not depend on fossil fuels for the manufacture of pesticides or fertilizers, and is thus sustainable in a time when those fuels are expensive or in short supply. Also, according to Elaine Ingham, it requires less labor and uses water more efficiently.

Origin and Development of Organic Growers of Michigan (OGM)

The founders of OGM, John and Judy Yaeger, sent out a letter proposing an informal organizational meeting of organic farmers in Southwest Michigan on January 30, 1973. About 40 people attended that meeting in Decatur, and they began organizing. By March the group had chosen its name: Organic Growers of Michigan Cooperative, Inc. The creation of OGM as a cooperative was deliberate and reflected the cultural importance of cooperation and sharing, including management tasks. Since a paid staff was thus unnecessary, membership dues were a modest $7.00 per year to begin with. By May the certification committee, chaired by Mary Appelhof, was working on certification standards. She, educated in biology, was an expert on earthworms and had written and published a very successful book called *Worms Eat My Garbage*. Since I was involved with the group from the beginning, my farm, the School of Homesteading, was one of the first six farms to be certified organic in that first year, and I remained active in the movement and "Certified Organic" as a farmer for over thirty years. We learned later that OGM was among the first to be organized in the United States, along with organic groups in Maine and California.

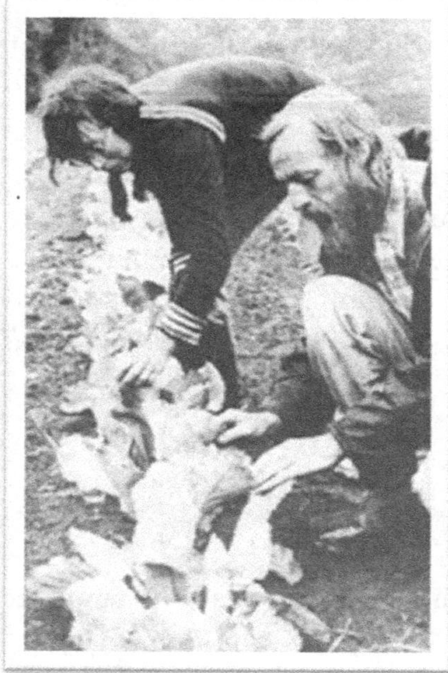

John and Judy Yaeger, founders of OGM

The Yaegers were a fairly young couple who had recently begun careers in the Chicago area. Both had their doctorates from the University of Chicago. John was teaching botany and Judy had a position as a researcher in psychology. They had come to southwest Michigan in search of a summer place and started raising vegetables with organic methods. They enjoyed country life so much that in a few years they gave up their jobs in Chicago and moved to their farm, which they called Peacewood. Their effort to organize a group of organic growers was prompted, in part, by their own desire to learn from fellow organic growers.

At the October meeting the founding members of OGM approved the by-laws and the Articles of Incorporation. The by-laws listed four purposes of OGM: to find markets for organically-grown produce, to facilitate the group purchase of supplies such as rock fertilizers, to develop a program and standards for the certification of organic produce, and to help educate members and the public about organic issues. The group was governed by a seven-member executive committee elected by grower members. By November not only was this committee functioning, but also seven other committees: purchasing, marketing, educational/ program, certification, membership, public relations, and newsletter. The purchasing committee had already coordinated the purchase and distribution of 180 tons of ground rock fertilizer which were delivered by rail to towns in the area. The proximity of Chicago to southwest Michigan made it an ideal market, but despite intense efforts, the group as a whole failed to develop a market in Chicago.

The internal organization of OGM got off to a great start. The achievements of the first year reflected high levels of enthusiasm among members. In its second year I was elected treasurer, and for 1974 I was asked to prepare two budgets: one for 50 members and one for 100 members. In fact the membership roster for 1974 listed 55 grower members and 53 supporting members in the Southwest chapter. Supporting members, including organic gardeners who produced only for household use and people who "believed in" the organic way, were welcome and helpful, but they could not vote or hold office. OGM was primarily for market growers who produced for sale. The distinction between growers and supporters was made only after intense and lengthy discussion. The growers for market felt it was necessary to maintain control over certification standards because their livelihood was at stake. Livestock was certified separately from land and the animals had to be fed at least 80% organically-produced feed. No additives, hormones or medicated feeds were permitted.

When OGM was organized in southwest Michigan there were already some organic gardening clubs, but OGM was the only organic organization deliberately organized to facilitate production for market. In April of 1974, however, another group was organized in the Grand Rapids area. The presence of another chapter prompted a revision of the by-laws of the founding Southwest Chapter to make provisions for other chapters to form under one set of by-laws. Article Two, on the OGM State Council, was added to the by-laws to facilitate inter-chapter coordination, but each chapter was expected to be fairly independent, so that the State Council would meet only once a year. The early organizers of OGM clearly cherished local control and did not envision becoming a state-wide political power. Later, when the first federal certification standards were released in 1997, OGM was not prepared to participate as a state-wide organization. But eventually the State Council became the main agent of OGM, so that the organization could speak with one voice.

Since we attended the monthly meetings of OGM regularly with our homesteading students in tow, we were quite visible in the local movement. During the 1970s we also raised vegetables and small fruit using organic methods and made sales at farmers markets in Kalamazoo and South Haven as well as on the farm. Sally was a committed and active member of OGM; in the 1980s, when interest in OGM waned as rapidly as it had grown during the 1970s, it was she who sent a letter to all members of our chapter inviting them to a reorganization meeting. Her effort was successful and the Southwest chapter was reinvigorated. Another factor that kept the group interested was the newsletter edited by Pat Whetham, *Michigan Organic News*. Still another was the active participation of a large grower unit (an 1800 acre cattle farm between Cassopolis and Niles) owned by John and Merrill Clark, who shared their expertise in many meetings of organic growers and eaters in the area.

Our lives became busier in 1976 when Joe Filonowitz came out of the Detroit area with money and the desire to organize a land trust. He had already organized one in North Carolina. We co-organized a group which was recognized by the Internal Revenue Service as a tax exempt charitable organization under section 501(c)(3) of its code. Joe and I agreed that we were doing this so our students would have land on which to start a farm. Although the potential availability of land did not tempt young people who were still completing their education, Joe did buy a farm and donated it to Michigan Land Trustees (MLT); it was called the Land Trust Homesteading Farm. MLT eventually provided support for the Homesteading program I got started as part of Environmental Studies at Western Michigan University, and my stepson Jon Towne eventually stepped in to serve as instructor of the course on the Land Trust Farm. He and his wife Bobbi Martindale later made an offer and bought the farm and continue to live there, across the street from our land.

In the early 1980s I used my relationship with Environmental Studies to ask them to do some research through the "Science for Citizens Program," on behalf of OGM and in response to a series of questions proposed by John Yaeger who was then serving as certification chair. I wrote a preamble to that "Science for Citizens" report entitled "Ethics and Values implicit in Organic Farming" to describe our central concerns as organic farmers. I included the fact that, according to David Pimentel in a *BioScience* article, crop loss due to insect damage had doubled since the 1940s even though the use of chemical insecticides increased tenfold in that time and was poisoning the land and our food.

During the later 1980s I became more active in OGM administration and was elected to chair the Southwest chapter in about 1987. During this time Sally was the secretary. Later, in the 1990s, I served as secretary. During these years Sally also edited the newsletter. In the late 1980s I was named as the chapter representative to the State Council and continued in that role for several years. Any business that required coordination between chapters, such as agreement on a common set of certification standards, was carried out by the State Council. I served as chair of the State Council for several years starting in 1989. This position made me painfully aware of the decline of interest and participation by members in OGM during these years. Fewer people were willing to take responsibility for the business of the group. As volunteers "burned out," we felt the need for funding or a grant to hire paid staff members.

Another factor that made life difficult for the group was the release of organic certification standards by the United States Department of Agriculture in 1997. At the outset many of the small farmers who started OGM were pleased both with the recognition of organic methods by the federal government and with the possibility that the government would enforce one set of standards. But when the first set of standards was released organic producers and eaters were outraged. The standards proposed to include genetically modified organisms, sewage sludge, and irradiation as organic. The outcry against these three was said to be the biggest protest the USDA ever heard from citizens. The revised standards deleted these three and the final standards were released in 2000 and implemented in 2002. Although OGM had evolved as an independent certifying agent, it now had to be accredited by the federal government and that proved to be very difficult. Although the certifying committee of OGM worked for several years to be accredited, and in effect separated the State Council as the certifying agency from the chapters of OGM, members of OGM seemed to have lost interest in the whole process and it was decided to dissolve OGM in 2006. Several other certifying agencies had emerged to certify organic growers.

Origins of Michigan Organic Food and Farm Alliance

Those of us who had been working with the State Council of OGM, which I chaired for several years starting in 1989, had already recognized that as members lost interest in working for OGM as volunteers, we needed to restructure the organization. Merrill Clark and I agreed that we needed an organizational structure that could receive funds from foundations. We tried to change the by-laws of OGM so it could be recognized as a charitable organization, but we were advised that this would not work because OGM was a business organization. Since we could not change OGM, we worked to organize a new group that could be approved by the Internal Revenue Service as a tax-exempt organization under section 501(c)(3) of the tax code. After consulting with several leaders in OGM, Merrill Clark and I called a meeting in October of 1991 to form a new organization. Legal costs and the IRS filing fee were provided by a memorial fund in honor of my wife Sally who, before she died in 1990, requested that OGM be designated to receive memorial gifts and hold any funds so received to start a new organization.

The new organization was originally called "Michigan Organic Growers Advancement Project" and it was incorporated in the State of Michigan in January of 1992. It was approved by the IRS as a tax-exempt charitable organization in June of 1992 under section 501(c)(3). The new board, which I, having called the meeting, served as chair for five years, were all members of OGM and efforts were made to schedule meetings on the same day and place as meetings of the State Council of OGM. In fact the board of the new organization included many of the movers and shakers from OGM.

*Sally Kaufman, **1929-1990***

During the next year the name of the group was changed to "Michigan Organic Food and Farm Alliance" (MOFFA). A new mission statement was adopted to reflect the broader concerns of the organization: "MOFFA promotes the development of food systems that rely on organic methods and that revitalize and sustain local communities." These actions represented a small shift away from OGM since members of OGM were slow to support MOFFA, but the main reason was the board's concern for the development of local food systems. These include but are more than organic agriculture. Laura DeLind, a faculty member at Michigan State University, had been arguing, quite correctly, that MOFFA should move beyond the commercial aspects of organic farming toward a consideration of social and ecological issues. MOFFA's "local food" logo, which was created by Laura DeLind, was made available for MOFFA's use during this time.

Local Food logo by Laura DeLind

In 1994 Laura DeLind began editing a new newsletter, *Michigan Organic Connections.* It was continued with different editors and replaced Pat Whetham's *Michigan Organic News.* Laura DeLind's academic connections made it possible for her to begin coordinating the "organic day" in the annual Agriculture and Natural Resources Week at Michigan State University in 1993. She secured nationally-known speakers and coordinated the workshops for several years. Of special value was her selection of speakers who were of interest to eaters of organic food, and not just to producers. This helped to grow the market for organic food.

A major project, intended to be an annual event, was the Michigan Organic Harvest Festival. This involved contacting organic growers to provide food and of course speakers and workshops on relevant topics. It was a very demanding task for MOFFA board members. But during the early years of this century other groups in different cities worked with the board to make it happen. Annual Harvest Festivals were offered first in the Detroit area, then in the Grand Rapids area, and I was able to organize a third in the Kalamazoo area. I learned from other successful efforts to work with local groups and we began an annual event in 2003, at Tillers International near Scotts, Michigan, east of Kalamazoo, which has continued until this writing. Tillers had just settled in on a large farm with space for public gatherings. It was here that they headquartered their technology-transfer work to African countries. As it became a community Harvest Fest the word "organic" was gradually lost from the title, but it functioned in the program.

Although no really large grant proposals by MOFFA to foundations have been successful, many smaller grants have kept the organization functioning. It has served, probably better than OGM did, as the educational arm of the organic movement in Michigan, especially through the efforts of Laura DeLind. Several commercial certifying agencies had emerged to do the job of certification according to the standards set by the National Organic Standards Board (NOSB). This board includes a representation of all interested parties, including farmers, processors, scientists, and organic industry representatives. Many of the organic growers who started the organic organizations in Michigan were alarmed by the growing power of big, corporate organics, and began to feel that the recognition of organic production by the USDA was the kiss of death.

Although I am no longer closely involved with MOFFA, it seems to be maintaining its integrity. It still speaks for small-scale organic growers and raises questions about corporate attempts to take over the organic industry. How it will react when corporate arrogance seriously damages organic standards remains to be seen.

Writing About Organic Issues

One of the things academicians do is write papers, read them at conferences to other academicians and, hopefully, get them published. This is the kind of activity that my shift from the university to the farm caused me to neglect the most, and it did irreparable harm to my career, both on an academic level and in the organic movement. From 1973 to 1982 I did not write any academic papers or travel to professional conferences. I did, of course, write short articles for local newsletters of Organic Growers of Michigan, Michigan Organic Food and Farm Alliance, or Michigan Land Trustees, as well as short papers for delivery on campus or at local events. This writing helped to get me grounded in the emerging field of sustainable agriculture studies, and as we had fewer students on the farm in the 1980s, I was able to accompany my friend Ken Dahlberg to a few of these conferences.

The first of these conferences was in 1982 at the University of Florida; it was entitled "Agriculture, Change and Human Values" and was funded by the W. K. Kellogg Foundation. The title of my paper was "Visions for the Future of Agriculture." The second, in 1984, was an international conference sponsored by Michigan State University and the International Federation of Organic Agriculture Movements (IFOAM). Here I read a paper based on my literary studies that was designed to articulate cultural values that could motivate new farmers toward sustainable agriculture. It was entitled "The Pastoral Ideal and Sustainable Agriculture," but it was not well understood or accepted by agricultural scientists who assumed the only worthwhile motivation was the farmer's desire to make money. But I did enjoy evenings of beer drinking with the

German "organic pope" Hartmut Vogtmann. Tom Edens, a MSU prof who was one of the organizers of the conference, also arranged a bus tour for the international attendees, and when they spent a couple of hours on our farm, I offered them home-brewed beer along with a short tour.

The third conference, in 1986, was at the University of California in Santa Cruz and was sponsored by its Agroecology Program and IFOAM. (As a result of this connection to IFOAM I was able to convince OGM to become a member of IFOAM, but dues were expensive and the membership was not sustained until MOFFA joined IFOAM again under John Biernbaum's leadership in 2017.) The paper I read in California was entitled "From Domination to Cooperation: Ethical and Economic Motivations Toward Sustainable Food Production Systems." I always reported on these conferences at subsequent organic growers' meetings and I think these reports were more influential there than at the academic meetings.

As part of our outreach as a School of Homesteading, we, along with Michigan Land Trustees, sponsored various workshops and meetings open to the public on our farm. On several occasions we hosted field days for OGM, some of which were attended by 200 to 300 people. One of these was funded by a grant from MOFFA in 1998, and was designed to attract conventional farmers to produce for the organic market, and it attracted about 250 people. Many of these events generated reports in newspapers and magazines, in addition to earlier articles about the School of Homesteading and organic farming. Sally saved nearly a hundred of these reports in large albums. In March of 1975 we were featured in a long article on the new homesteading schools in Rodale's *Organic Gardening and Farming* magazine. And in 1984 I made the cover of *The New Farm*, another Rodale publication. When I walked into the feed store soon after that I was greeted with "here comes the cover boy." The article, "Evolution of a Small Farm," by

Paul Gilk, was published as a rebuttal to Earl Butz, a Secretary of Agriculture, whose message to farmers was "Get big or get out."

I really appreciated the fact that Paul Gilk wrote that article and got it published. He is an old friend I met years ago at a conference in Indiana; now he lives and writes in a log cabin in northern Wisconsin. We discovered we had similar backgrounds and read many of the same radical books, such as *Life Against Death* by Norman Brown. He is both a diligent and excellent writer of over eight published books. Several years ago my academic friend, Ken Dahlberg, Paul and I laid plans for the publication of a quarterly magazine we called *Eutopian Journal* in which we would seek and publish articles on living in a good place instead of the utopian noplace of industrial society. But we failed to get the funding to get started.

Late in 2004 I was asked to prepare and deliver the keynote address at the Annual Organic Conference scheduled for March 5, 2005, at Michigan State University in East Lansing. I prepared the paper well over a month in advance and got some advice on how to improve it. I titled the paper "Organic Farming and the Organic Way of Life." Then, a week before the conference, I came down with a flu which totally destroyed my voice. As luck would have it, I did recover my voice the day before the conference and managed the delivery in fine shape. The audience seemed appreciative, perhaps because I had some status as the "elder statesman" of the organic movement in Michigan. I have to admit that being asked to give that keynote address was one of the most gratifying experiences I have enjoyed.

Paul Gilk

I wrote a book in 2007-2008, *Adapting to the End of Oil: Toward an Earth-Centered Spirituality.* It was based on the "peak oil" movement of that time, before fracking made much more oil available and lowered the price. But I did try to emphasize the fact that burning oil and other fossil fuels adds carbon dioxide, a greenhouse gas, that warms the atmosphere to catastrophic levels. Since I was slow to find a commercial publisher, I impatiently had it self-published and as a result it failed to gain much circulation.

A few years later, when Judy Yaeger, who was the founder of OGM with her husband John, came back to Michigan from Texas where she had been living, I was able to arrange a conversation with her, including reminiscences about the early years of the movement, in the Decatur Library where OGM had its meetings for several years. Ken Dahlberg helped to film the conversation, now called *The Roots of OGM*, and after it was edited and shortened a bit, it is available for viewing at http://michiganorganic.org/roots-of-ogm.

On the strength of this video I began to imagine the whole history of the organic movement in Michigan documented on a series of videos. Since books are more economical, in about 2011 I drafted an outline for a book on the organic movement in Michigan. But I needed someone with the requisite computer skills to help with the book, and the editing project I envisioned languished until Julia Christianson volunteered to help. She was working part-time as MOFFA's administrative staff and had already volunteered to help with archiving a variety of papers from the organic movement. As she read those papers she got a birds-eye view of the how the movement had developed in Michigan, and we decided to be co-editors of a book we called *The Organic Movement in Michigan.* In 2016 we contacted people who had been active in the movement and asked them to contribute. In May of 2017 the book was published by MOFFA, which is designated as the recipient of any profits.

The published version included most of the topics and writers that I originally envisioned, but not all of them since some of the original activists had moved on. And it included relevant topics and writers suggested by Julia. Laura DeLind provided a striking cover for it. Although the book is more than a simple history of the organic movement, it does cover the origin and development of OGM and MOFFA. Part III, the longest part of the book, is devoted to a variety of other organic groups and activities. Part IV, entitled "Organic Farming: Now More Important than Ever," begins with one of the issues that the organic movement faces: how the organic industry is growing at the expense of the grass-roots farmers and groups that started the movement. Some of the problems this creates are discussed in the next section of this chapter.

Finally, in the last few years I have written and published articles on how organic farming could mitigate climate change. Many appeared in *Green Horizons* magazine. The most recent of these is the final chapter in our book, *The Organic Movement in Michigan.* Each of my papers, in one way or another, argues against technological solutions to the excess of carbon dioxide in the atmosphere, and for the recognition that carbon dioxide is a vital nutrient for plant growth, and through organic farming it can find its way back into the soil from whence it came via photosynthesis.

Along with a number of non-profits in which we retain membership, Barbara and I are supporting members of a rather unique local organization in our neighboring town of South Haven. It is a museum headquartered in the house where Liberty Hyde Bailey, the famous agrarian and horticultural scientist, was born. Its board sponsors local programs of various kinds and asked me to give public talks a couple of times. They are a lively group of local citizens, proud of our native son.

Some Current Threats to Organic Farming

Ronnie Cummins, director of the Organic Consumers Association, published an article in the February 2018 issue of *AcresUSA* which reported that the National Organic Standards Board voted to allow growers of hydroponic vegetables to label their produce "organic." This was done despite the campaign to "keep the soil in organic" that had been gaining support in recent years. On the first page of this chapter I included a paragraph on one definition of organic, "feed the soil to feed the plant." This definition, which may be too simplistic, focuses on the biological process of plant growth and clearly distinguishes it from the process in conventional agriculture which emphasizes feeding the plant the necessary minerals. According to the recent ruling by the NOSB, hydroponic agriculture provides soluble "organic" fertilizers in solution to feed the plants and thus is permitted to bypass the biological processes in which nutrients are provided by the organisms in the soil. This recent vote by the NOSB illustrates the growing power of the large corporations who produce by far the largest share of organic food. So-called "Big Organic" is now, according to Cummins, "dictating the policies of the USDA's National Organic Program." They are able to do so, in collusion with the USDA, because the USDA is more supportive of growth in the economy than of healthy food. If it appears to support healthy food through the National Organic Program, it is willing, in spite of that, to subvert that support by failing to uphold the organic law that should govern all producers of organic food. This has been documented repeatedly by organizations such as the Cornucopia Institute, which has shown, for example, how large dairy farms do not provide pasture for their cattle as the law requires.

The campaign to keep the soil in organic production has been a response to the earlier illegal certification of hydroponic growing methods. In the Winter, 2016, issue of the Cornucopia newsletter, an article reported on the practice of some certifying organizations to certify hydroponic production as organic, even though it clearly violates the intent of the original legislation. This issue also reported on how the NOSB was being stacked with corporate employees posing as organic farmers. This seems to have been the strategy that made possible the recent vote to make hydroponics legal in organic production.

Cummins argues for the preservation of the integrity of the organic production system because the alternative, non-organic industrial food, is making us in America sick. Organic food constitutes only about 5% of the food supply in this country, but it is growing as increasing numbers of citizens are aware of how industrial food, with, as Cummins says, "genetically engineered ingredients, pesticides, antibiotics and other animal drug residues, pathogens, feces, hormone-disrupting chemicals, toxic sludge, slaughterhouse waste, chemical additives, preservatives, irradiation-derived radiolytic particles, and a host of other hazardous allergens and toxins" is making us sick. Cummins goes on to warn that within a decade "these diet- and environment-related diseases, heavily subsidized under our Big Pharma / chemical / genetically-engineered / factory farm system, will likely bankrupt Medicare and the entire $3.5 trillion (and rising) U.S. healthcare system." Of course this medical system has also appeared as a big business tempting to investors.

What is to be done? To preserve the integrity of the organic system, Cummins and his Organic Consumers Association have joined with the Rodale Institute to promote a new third-party Regenerative Organic Agriculture (RO) Certification. They propose that it would be added to and appear next to the current "USDA Organic" label, based on higher standards for soil health, land management, animal welfare and farmer and worker fairness. It would go beyond USDA Organic. There are other proposals for a better organic certification, but at this time the situation is in flux.

One emphasis in the Regenerative Organic standard that I find particularly significant is its energy-conserving awareness. Despite our current president's denial, millions of Americans realize that the increasing level of greenhouse gas pollution in the atmosphere, of which, says Cummins, "44 to 57 percent ... comes from degenerative food, farming and land-use practices," threatens the earth with global warming. The burning of fossil fuels adds more greenhouse gases. The new Regenerative Organic Certification standard makes the mitigation of global warming an important part of its certification standard and emphasizes renewable energy. This is generally implied in any promotion of organic farming, which thrives on the sequestration of carbon in plants and soil. And it is this that is denied in the hydroponic production of vegetables.

But is this new regenerative emphasis adequate in a corporate-controlled society? I remain dubious about its long-term success. The Bible tells us that "the love of money is the root of all evils." In this country the love of money has been institutionalized in a corporate system designed mainly to make money. The National Organic Program is now a bureaucracy under the Agricultural Marketing Service of the USDA. The power of Big Organic will find other ways to cut corners to make more money; in collusion with the USDA it may even try to forbid this supplemental certification standard.

The radical solution is to go back to where we began in this book with the new homesteading movement, or back to a pre-industrial society on a cultural level. There is evidence that this back-to-the-land movement did contribute to the beginnings of the organic movement. Homesteading implies self-provisioning, especially in food, and this can be accomplished in both rural and urban settings. It certainly also implies low-tech, organic methods of food production and preservation. More generally, it implies a process Paul Hawken called "disintermediation"—living, as much as possible, outside of the market economy, the great mediator between production and consumption, and focusing on the household economy. But only in the last couple of decades have I been able to see, in the context of the threat of climate change, that in order to curtail the emission of greenhouse gases we have to manage without fossil fuels.

And this means that we will manage with a drastically reduced industrial system of production and distribution. This had already been one of the main themes in my life, and it will be featured in the final chapter, as it summarizes the chief concerns of my life.

Chapter VI: Food Systems: Sacred, Profane and Demonic

(This was originally a lecture sponsored by Fair Food Matters in Kalamazoo and delivered in August of 2003. It summarized my thinking about food issues in relation to religion then, and it can remain unchanged to express my position now. Readers are advised that references are to events as they happened in 2003.)

A little over thirty years ago I published a scholarly article on the new homesteading movement. Since I was already living on a small farm west of Kalamazoo and raising food for the family, I felt I was part of that homesteading movement. This was in the time of the back-to-the-land movement and my students were enthusiastic about self-reliance on the land. They asked me to teach them the arts and skills of self-reliance; thus the idea of the school of homesteading was born.

When I asked my colleagues in the Religion Department for a half-time leave of absence from classroom teaching, they asked me what self-provisioning in food had to do with the study of religion. I was not able to provide a satisfactory answer then. Now I think I can. But thirty years ago there was, compared to now, very little awareness of "food systems." Food was simply a part of agriculture, and although environmentalists were beginning to think about alternatives to chemically-dependent agribusiness, a separate focus on food systems was only gradually beginning to emerge. One of the first references to "food systems" I remember was the title of a book in 1983, *Sustainable Food Systems.* I think it is significant that awareness of food systems emerged when corporate control and the industrialization of food and agriculture began to take over and crowd out small farms and locally-owned grocery stores. My work with MOFFA, Michigan Organic Food and Farm Alliance, also prompted me to learn about the global food system as we worked for local food systems.

Sycamores, 2012

Food systems range from simple to highly intermediated and complex. Raising food in your back yard, processing and preparing and eating it, and composting food wastes is a simple food system. (It only becomes complex when you try to do it!) Buying food in a supermarket may seem like a simple process: you simply buy it and eat it. But such food is the product of a capital- and energy-intensive corporate food system, dependent on transportation and a high degree of processing. Moreover, this food has lost its intrinsic value as nourishment. It has been transformed into a commodity and is produced for only one reason: to make money. Such food can no longer be seen as a sacred reality.

It may help us to understand how food can participate in the sacred if we examine how food was seen in archaic or pre-modern societies. The great historian of religion, Mircea Eliade, wrote a book called *Patterns in Comparative Religion.* The chapter on vegetation is twice as long as other chapters because there are so many examples of the regenerative power in nature. Plants, especially trees, are charged with the power of the sacred. They lose their leaves and die and are regenerated in spring. Thus trees can be seen as sacred symbols expressing the regenerative power of nature. The sacred is power. Rites and symbols and myths are religious because they relate us to the power of the sacred and help us participate in that power.

Eliade's chapter on agriculture explains how farming was such an important religious rite because now humans were intervening directly in the regenerative power of nature. It has been argued that women invented horticulture. While the men were out hunting, the women, as they were gathering, noticed that food grew where seeds were scattered. Soon women were scattering seeds and agriculture was born.

It is true that because of the association of woman, earth and fertility, women were essential to the raising of crops. In some places naked maidens went into the fields to show the plowmen where to plow. Or, in many cultures there was ritual copulation on the plowed ground, the man with his phallic spade and the woman identified with the furrow. Such rituals, and many others, more orgiastic, were believed to enhance the fertility of the soil. I could go on to describe them in greater detail, but this is a family-oriented program so I will stop here. But the raising of food required the power of the sacred and food itself was sacred because it assured the regeneration of life. This worldview persisted in peasant societies well into the nineteenth society.

During the last three or four centuries the Enlightenment and the Scientific Revolution gradually changed the sacred understanding of agriculture and food. We learned how plants grow. We learned that they need nitrogen, phosphorus and potassium, along with trace minerals, and we learned how to add these elements to the soil to make plants grow. If weeds or insects interfered with our plants we made pesticides to kill them. We no longer needed to rely on those "obscene" rituals to protect our plants or to assure the fertility of the soil. The sense of the organic unity of nature was replaced by a mechanistic view. Personal involvement was replaced by scientific technique. Wherever people adopted a scientific world-view, a sense for the regenerative power of nature was lost. They moved from the sacred to the profane.

But the worship of power did not simply end. Rather, (and this is extremely important to understand) as people lost a sense for the sacred power in nature they gained a new respect for the power to control nature. The scientist, in his white lab coat, replaced the priest or shaman as our sacred hero. The mythical man on his tractor, and his little woman in the kitchen, are sure they have better living through chemistry. They no longer have to do the onerous work of raising food; they can go to the supermarket and choose, from hundreds of brands, food that is cheap and tasty. They are consumers of commodities in what seems to be a totally desacralized world.

I say "seems to be" because the worship of power has not ended. But the object of that worship is no longer the sacred regenerative power in nature. Most people in the modern world worship the power to control nature, and this is a diabolical power. Remember how Faust, our modern culture hero, sought power from the Devil to control and manipulate nature. Remember how Jesus, after fasting in the wilderness, was tempted by the Devil who offered him power in return for adoration. The Devil had the power to offer; worldly power is demonic. Our technological ability has freed us from reliance on divine powers. In our ignorance and short-sightedness we have come to rely on demonic powers. During the past quarter-century or so, this demonic power has made a quantum leap in economic concentration. This is the power of trans-national corporations, who hire scientists and politicians to do their will. They now control much of the world. 52 of the 100 largest economies in the world are business corporations, and many are involved in food and agriculture, the biggest industry of all.

Why should these corporations be thought of as demonic? I have already mentioned the fact that they seek power to control and change the natural or created order. Genetic engineering is a current example. Barbara Kingsolver called this a fist in the eye of God because it threatens the natural biodiversity on which the stability of ecosystems depend. When Percy Schmeiser, the Canadian canola grower, spoke at the Organic Conference last March in East Lansing, he suggested that bio-tech corporations like Monsanto might deliberately allow genetically modified seeds to contaminate natural seeds so that their market for genetically modified seeds can increase. Whether Monsanto's seeds contaminated Schmeiser's fields by accidental drift or otherwise, Monsanto sued him because they had a patent on the seeds through intellectual property rights.

The fact that corporations seek to control nature for profit is also demonic. As Norman O. Brown explained, "modern secularism, and its companion, Protestantism, do not usher in an era in which human consciousness is liberated from inhuman powers, or the natural world is liberated from supernatural manifestations; the essence of the Protestant (or capitalist) era is that the power over the world has passed from God to God's ape, the Devil ... The money complex is the demonic, and the demonic is God's ape; the money complex is therefore the heir to and substitute for the religious complex, an attempt to find God in things." Brown is using mythical imagery here, (as I do) to describe cultural dynamics because only mythic stories (in which divine beings interact with humans) can convey the magnitude of current cultural changes in the human condition. The symbol of the demonic need not be understood literally to mean that there is an actual supernatural being out there.

Another characteristic of corporations as demonic structures was brought into focus by the twentieth century philosophical theologian Paul Tillich, who revived the concept of the demonic as manifest in and through secular activities. He argued that the demonic is a structure of evil primarily because it arrogates ultimate power, or unconditional status, or unlimited expansion to itself and thus refuses to recognize any limitation or judgment upon itself. While corporations may not be inherently evil, they are structured, by law, to make a profit for their shareholders. And as they make a profit they gain power. Money is power and power corrupts. Absolute power tends to corrupt absolutely. As a result of this power and insatiable greed, the rich get richer and the poor get poorer. The top fifth of people in the world receive 82.7% of total world income, while the bottom three fifths receives only 5.4%.

This was in 1992, and the disparity in income has grown since then.

I will conclude this section on corporations by listing several specific examples which illustrate how we can speak of the global supermarket as a demonic food system. First is the problem of globalization itself, especially as it destroys local cultures and exacerbates the detachment of people from their local ecosystems. People in developed societies have already lost any sense of dependence on local ecosystems. They are "distanced" from their food, both literally and metaphorically. Trans-national corporations are busy transforming subsistence cultures around the world into consumer cultures. There will no longer be enough people who know or care about the preservation of biodiversity in local ecosystems. In addition to this we must charge agricultural corporations with pollution of air, water, and soil as they externalize the environmental costs of production. The recent war in Iraq reminded us that corporations need cheap oil to transport food around the world, and that adds to global warming. We face the threat of ecological collapse because of what demonic food corporations are doing to make money.

Second is another consequence of globalization as transnational corporations enclose and privatize common lands in Third World countries. Displaced peasants are lucky if they can be hired to produce crops for export. Most lose subsistence opportunities for self-provisioning and employment as they crowd into shanty towns around urban centers. This is often the result of "structural adjustment programs" in which the World Bank requires indebted nations to produce crops for export so they can get cash to repay debts. Because of low wages and exploitation of workers, food can be imported into this country cheaper than it can be grown here. Apple orchards are being bulldozed in Van Buren county because it is cheaper to import apples from China or Chile, the largest supplier of off-season fruits and vegetables to Europe and the United States where 50% of the crop is controlled by a handful of transnational corporations. Such imported food, incidentally, is often produced without the environmental regulations that protect us from pesticide residues in this country.

Third, in addition to the exploitation of cheap labor, there is actual slavery in food production for the transnational corporations. Gary Paul Nabhan reported that 27 million people are enslaved in the global food system. The New Yorker magazine recently published an exposé of how migrant workers are enslaved in tomato production in Florida. The corporate strategy is to impoverish workers to such an extent that they are willing to work for food. Where profit is the only consideration there is no concern for the health or well-being of workers.

Fourth, the billions of dollars spent on advertising lure innocent or ignorant customers to buy processed food even though it is inferior to natural whole food. An example from several years ago is the three to four thousand babies that died each day because they were fed (improperly, to be sure) on infant formula made by Nestle instead of breast milk. Brewster Kneen quite correctly called corporations like Nestle "murderers." Demonic corporations profit by deception and outright lies.

Although books have been written to detail many more corporate abuses in the pursuit of profit, we have enough examples to recognize the corporate food system as not just profane but demonic. Most poor people, in this country and elsewhere, live in a world where they are confronted by hostile powers which seek their own ends at the expense of those already impoverished. Programs such as NAFTA and WTO, which transfer global governance from democratic governments to corporations, are pushed through the legislative process by corporations who buy and sell politicians. Corporations have more power than governments, and we should bear in mind that the political corollary of demonic corporations is fascism. A dictionary definition of fascism provided by Thom Hartmann can help us recognize our current government: "fascism, a system of government that exercises a dictatorship of the extreme right, typically through the merging of state and business leadership, together with belligerent nationalism." Although some of us may be critical of George Bush and his policies, polls show that the masses still love George Bush because he and his corporate friends so brazenly manifest the power to control the world. The worship of power is alive and well! The masses also love the fact that Bush has the power to lie with impunity. So I am using these extreme words, demonic and fascist, to help us avoid facile optimism as we think about the possibility of reforming the system we live in.

And I should emphasize that we are in the system. All of us, when we purchase corporate food or eat in a fast-food restaurant, participate in a demonic food system. Yes, most of us are also demon-possessed, especially when we are shopping.

I don't think we can reform the system, and I think it is wrong to seek power to overthrow it. But I think it will collapse because it is not sustainable as it exploits nature and human beings in its single-minded quest for profit. Because corporate control is so total, its collapse could cause even more massive suffering and chaos than it has caused in its success. Or we may see a gradual disintegration. In either case, we can prepare for the end of the demonic food system by assessing our resources for an alternative. The nation-wide movement toward local organic food systems could be an important part of the emerging alternative. At this point, however, this system is still too small to be much of a threat and so corporations have left it alone. But it is likely that as the organic food supply does grow it will continue to be co-opted by corporate control. So it may be that small-scale local food systems are more promising as a viable alternative food system. Above all, we should be concerned about the moral and religious values which alternative food systems reflect or embody.

In our world shaped by the Judeo-Christian tradition I can think of two types of sacred food systems: either the system is in conformity with an established religious tradition or it is in harmony with an ecosystem conceived as a sacred reality. The first is the Judeo-Christian emphasis on stewardship. The creation myths in the book of Genesis have helped countless generations understand themselves in their world. It was a world created by God who then created humans in His own image and gave them dominion over other creatures. God also (in the second story) put Adam in the garden and instructed him to till it and keep it. So here we have the idea of stewardship: humans are given dominion but also responsibility. This is an anthropocentric ethic in which humans are led to think of themselves as separate from, but responsible for, their natural environment. Just as God was above nature, manifest in history, so humans are above nature and active in making history. In this story God is the absentee landlord who has put humans in charge.

I have known many Christians who have consciously and deliberately sought to live and work as farmers in accordance with the ethic of stewardship, even when it meant simply being more careful. Or stewardship may be appropriated in a more secular context by farmers working toward more sustainable methods, such as the members of the Michigan Agricultural Steward Association. There is also the Land Stewardship Association in the Great Plains states which promotes an ethic of soil conservation. These are worthwhile efforts, but it is important to see that they operate on an ethical level. I do not think these farmers would describe their efforts as constituting a "sacred food system," and I am quite sure they would not think of food as sacred. In the Judeo-Christian tradition God alone is the sacred reality. Nature is good because God created it, but it is not itself regarded as sacred. God may be thanked for the food, but the food is not sacred. By being given dominion, humans are separate from nature. While they may take responsibility for nature, they will not easily feel kinship with other species or feel themselves as being part of an ecosystem.

These comments should not be construed as a negative attitude toward what remains, for most of us, the dominant religious tradition. I have the highest respect for any number of thinkers and writers who work explicitly in a Christian context. I am thinking of E. F. Schumacher and a more recent writer, Brewster Kneen, whose book, *From Land to Mouth* is the clearest exposition of the concept of food systems. Conventional Christianity is simply the kind of religion that thrusts its adherents into the secular world where they are called to live in a morally-responsible manner. At the same time, it must be acknowledged that Christianity is very easily assimilated by secular culture. Very few Christian farmers who may talk about stewardship on Sunday have shifted away from conventional chemically-dependent farming methods on Monday. To this extent they have moved from the sacred to the profane. Some Christians have changed to organic farming methods, but it is not clear to me that they did so for explicitly religious reasons. The organic orientation can also be assimilated from contemporary culture, or these farmers may be in quest of higher prices for their produce.

It is easier to interpret and evaluate the religious dimensions in organic farming. My 30 plus years of association with organic farmers has made it abundantly clear that organic farming and gardening is a kind of incipient religious movement even though it may not be recognized as such by the farmers themselves. Organic farming began as a reaction to the use of chemical fertilizers as tractors replaced draft animals. In Germany Rudolf Steiner, founder of Biodynamic agriculture, wrote the first book on organic farming in 1924 as part of his quasi-religious Anthroposophy. As they challenged the use of chemical fertilizers, and later chemical pesticides, organic farmers went against the grain of conventional agriculture. They tried to work in harmony with nature. They worked in faith as they trusted in micro-organisms in the soil to feed plants long before science confirmed their intuition. At one of the first organic meetings I attended I heard the farmers tell each other: "yeah, feed the soil, not the plant." It took me a while to figure that out, but it remains one of the maxims of organic farming and, as it implies a holistic rather than a reductionistic orientation, it brings back that sense of organic unity that preceded the Scientific Revolution.

Rudolf Steiner

Rudolf Steiner, incidentally, did explicitly relate his lectures on agriculture to the sacred. Although I cannot remember this exactly (I read the book 20 years ago) Steiner wrote many pages detailing the ritual of making compost starter. Since both terrestrial and celestial influences were necessary, Steiner explained that it was necessary to take some cow manure, put some in a cow's horn and some in a cow's hoof, let it decompose for a year, mix with water at a certain phase of the moon, stir it clockwise and counter-clockwise for a certain number of times and then add it to the compost where it would function in a homeopathic manner. These exacting rituals were intended to change the food it produced so that the resulting food would change the eater. Steiner was basically a religious thinker, and I agree with critics of the biodynamic method who see these rituals as a regression to magical thinking.

To think and work as an organic farmer or gardener is one way of moving from an anthropocentric to a biocentric orientation. This is really quite revolutionary and it is interesting to notice that practice precedes theory in this instance. There is evidence for a broader and deeper cultural shift here as practices such as recycling and organic gardening move people toward a new awareness and a new lifestyle. A rather light-hearted but basically serious article in the July issue of *Harper's* Magazine, "A Gospel According to the Earth," reflects on the possibility that a new eco-faith is emerging in Western societies. The article is an extended meditation on a series of words such as "compost. global warming. off the grid. pollution. renewable. tree-sitting." and their conventional religious associations or implications in Christianity. So this author is implying that a change within Christianity is happening. As process theology based on the thought of Alfred North Whitehead taught us for at least 50 years, "the world is God's Body." Environmental concerns, which are widespread among common people everywhere, may gradually help us recognize ourselves as cells in that Body.

A couple of Christian thinkers have also been urging new ways of recovering a sense for cosmic sacrality. Matthew Fox has written about "creation spirituality," and argued that the conventional emphasis on personal sin and redemption was a distortion of the Christian gospel.

Thomas Berry similarly argued for a "New Story" which would incorporate the whole process of cosmic and biological evolution into our self-understanding. And the thought of Thomas Berry is fully grounded when he urges backyard organic gardening as the first step toward healing the earth.

Also in the early 1970s, as the organic movement was getting started in Michigan, a young poet and writer from Kentucky published a book of poems called *Farming: A Hand Book*. Now recognized as the foremost agrarian philosopher, Wendell Berry has also contributed enormously to the resurgence of this sense for the regenerative power of nature. The first poem in that book is called "The Man Born to Farming."

The grower of trees, the gardener, the man born to farming,
whose hands reach into the ground and sprout,
to him the soil is a divine drug. He enters into death
yearly, and comes back rejoicing. He has seen the light
lie down in the dung heap, and rise again in the corn.

Wendell Berry

Wendell Berry moves beyond the Christian ethic of stewardship as he celebrates the cyclical structure of time and the sacred power of nature, especially in his poetry.

Although Wendell Berry is an agrarian and has written countless essays on the values of small-scale farming, it is essential to remember that his emphasis is on subsistence farming, on the household economy, or, as he entitled one of his books, on *Home Economics*. This is an emphasis nearly always neglected by professional or scientific writers. But the backyard garden is the most ecological kind of food production possible. Any agro-ecological system will distort the ecosystem because, in order to derive a sustainable harvest from a piece of land it is necessary to provide some inputs. The cyclical processes of the ecosystem are thus disrupted and it begins to be a through-put process in which the decomposer organisms are bypassed. If we value the ecosystem as a sacred power which provides food for life, we should learn to live as consumer organisms in the system rather than consumers of the harvest who live outside of the system.

Illustration by Penny Kelly

I want to conclude with one more evidence of the resurgence of the sacred in the backyard garden. This is the reappearance of nature spirits in the garden. Many of you have probably read about the devas and elemental beings in the garden at Findhorn, in Scotland, where they helped the gardeners produce fabulous crops. This spring there was a lovely little article in the *Healing Garden Journal* about elves and fairies in the garden. And, of course, we have the fascinating book by local author Penny Kelly: *The Elves of Lily Hill Farm.* Although I, with my coarse sensibility and rational mind, lack the finesse to tune in to the vibrations that make such vision possible, I would like to see and sometimes I try.

Chapter VII: Resisting Climate Change

So far this book has reflected my more serious and scholarly self. It may continue to do so because my style of writing, carefully developed over the years, does not easily allow me to lapse into more colloquial or informal modes of expression. I seem to be stuck in the scholarly mode. But this is a superficial and false representation of who I am and how I lived my life. I was good at writing papers, but I probably never was a committed academic scholar. What serious scholar would give up a promising academic career to be a farmer? For example, even before we started the School of Homesteading I had written one theological essay which generated some favorable response from professional theologians, but I failed to follow through with more. I was too busy renovating a run-down small farm for the joy of it. Of course it was only a modest response from three scholars in the late 1960s, but it was a response to only one single essay. I should have carried on with more such essays, but I was too busy enjoying life on a new farm. My choice to do a School of Homesteading was also clearly done in a hedonistic context. I have almost always acted in a self-indulgent manner and did what felt right (and good) at the time. By this I mean that I did what felt good and also what I felt was right on a moral level.

And I have always enjoyed scholarly inquiry, first in my chosen field of religion and literature. Then, during the 1970s, my range of inquiry gradually shifted to religion and environmental studies, focusing on food and farming issues. Later I followed my interests more freely, as will be reviewed in this chapter. But I always loved the alternation of scholarly work inside with physical activity outside.

I should also acknowledge that I have been maladjusted for much of my life in regard to what most people see as reality. My 1972 essay on the new homesteading movement was subtitled "from utopia to eutopia," from the no-place of urban technological society to the good place on the land. This set the tone for a lot of things I have opposed, or for which I sought alternatives. This early essay opposed not only technological urban society but also conventional agribusiness and chemical inputs to raise crops. The homesteading experience made me conscious of other issues I opposed: the market economy, a commodity-intensive lifestyle, money, and energy-intensive economic growth seen as progress. This kind of opposition gradually led to a more comprehensive and conscious environmental critique in which I found myself more aware of the threat of climate change, as destructive agricultural practices and the burning of fossil fuels led to the accumulation of greenhouse gases in the atmosphere that is causing global warming. This reinforced my long-time distrust of industrial modes of production.

For the past ten years or so, after writing my book about the end of oil, I have been reading and thinking about how the excess carbon dioxide could be sequestered in the soil. I published about a half-dozen essays on this topic. Organic farming and gardening is central to this effort, as I argued in Chapter V. These articles were published locally in the newsletter of Michigan Land Trustees and in the *Green Horizon Magazine* with its small national circulation. They had titles such as "Against the Current: Efforts of a Transition Initiative," "Carbon Sequestration, Naturally," and "Hubris or Humus," in which hubris refers to the efforts of corporate entrepreneurs to solve climate change while humus is the humble effort of sequestering carbon in soil. These essays were based on a considerable body of scientific evidence.

Economic Issues Raised by Homesteading

In going through my files, I find notes and outlines for talks about homesteading. This was a popular topic during the 1970s, and I was a highly visible speaker on this topic because of the publicity that the School of Homesteading received in newspapers and magazines. I even wrote the first chapter of a book on homesteading which I called something like “The Urban Person’s Guide to Homesteading.” But there was such a surfeit of books on this topic during that time that I lost interest in adding to it and quit.

Since I started the School of Homesteading with a half-time leave of absence from the classroom at half my normal salary, our concern for economic issues was immediate as we adjusted to living with less money. We were ready for this to the extent that we felt confident we could raise the food we needed. But we were also ready for it because we had become increasingly disenchanted with the shoddy quality of consumer goods and ready to buy fewer things. We were ready to withdraw from the market economy as much as we could and to focus on the production of food, especially, for use in the household economy. And partly as a result of the new homesteading movement this was a growing phenomenon in the early 1970s. We learned more about this in a book by Scott Burns: *Home, Inc.: The Hidden Wealth and Power of the American Household*, published in 1975.

The book by Burns made us aware of the fact that, although it is a non-monetized economy, the household is a very large economy which in the 1960s produced goods and services valued at 300 billion dollars. He points out that if all the work done in the household were monetized it would be equal to the entire amount paid out in wages and salaries by every corporation in the United States. He also says that the assets commanded by households, worth more than a trillion dollars, produce an annual return in goods and services almost equal to the net profit of every corporation in the country. Whenever I filled out a census form it always instructed that production for use in the household should not be included, so the household economy is ignored by those who calculate the gross national product.

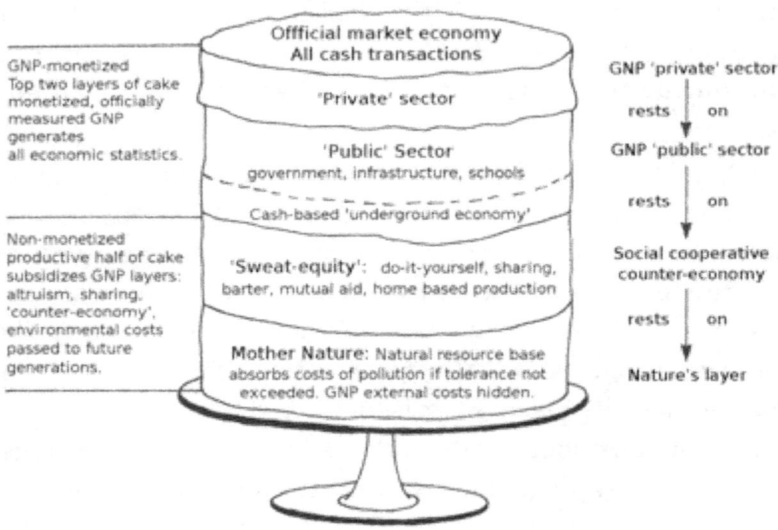

Total Productive System of an Industrial Society
(Three-layer cake with icing)
After Hazel Henderson, 1982

One of the topics that the book by Burns ignored, incidentally, was the energy crisis that occurred in the 1970s. We were made painfully aware of that in 1973 because we had to buy gasoline for the tractor—when it was available—in a 5-gallon pail. It was one of the reasons why we were motivated to start a School: food raised at home needs far less fossil fuel energy. The commercial food industry is the most energy-demanding industry, a problem to which we shall return. Burns also said very little about the books on limits to growth which were published starting in 1972, but he did alert his readers to the nature of the market economy as "a Faustian instrument, divorced from nature, with no inherent capacity for recognizing self-limiting factors." The market economy offers the freedom that comes from abolishing limits, but that only postpones, for a while, the eventual crash. Unlimited growth is not possible in a finite world with limited resources. The demonic nature of corporations, their refusal to recognize limits, was discussed in the previous chapter.

My commitment to homesteading, or production for use at home, was strengthened as I learned more about various economic arrangements. These included the self-provisioning household economy and economies of redistribution. Then, in the nineteenth century, the self-regulating market evolved and, as Karl Polanyi put it, "instead of economy being embedded in social relations, social relations are embedded in the economic system." This was indeed the "Great Transformation" which shaped the political and economic origins of our time. The tail was wagging the dog. This transformation was made possible by industrialization using fossil fuel energy to manufacture goods which are sold to consumers. It thrives on a dichotomy between production and consumption in which money is central, as that which mediates between them. In the process society was also transformed as the consumer had to make money with a job in order to buy the goods available in a commodity-intensive society.

The Great Transformation can also be seen as a stage in the enclosure of the commons. These enclosures occurred in the 18th and 19th centuries as land owners "enclosed" their land for raising sheep and expelled the peasants who had had traditional dwelling rights on the land. "Enclosure" is now a term used more generally for the transformation of the commons into resources for industrial production. Although Polanyi in his book discusses enclosure, he does not emphasize how the burning of fossil fuels in the process of industrialism creates enclosures. (He wrote the book in the mid-1940s). We now recognize that a commons, the air we breathe, is often polluted by industrial activities. More recently, we are anxious about the fact that the atmosphere has become a resource for the disposal of industrial wastes, a "sink" for the greenhouse gases given off as fossil fuels are burned.

There are many examples of how the industrial market encloses the commons. Polanyi was appalled by the fact that land and labor were transformed into commodities as they became parts of the market economy and thus subordinated to it, but labor and land are human beings and their environment. The enclosure of land continued with the enclosure of genes in genetic engineering. The crops raised with bio-technology also enclose the land itself as they pollute the crops not raised in the bio-tech way. The case of the Canadian canola grower, Percy Schmeiser, was mentioned in the previous chapter. He was sued by Monsanto when its genetically-modified canola drifted over his fields and contaminated his natural canola crop. Like many large corporations, Monsanto is more interested in making money than in raising food.

The central role of money in the market economy is an embarrassment to those who learn about it. To begin with, as Norman Brown explained in the previous chapter, money is rooted in the demonic. It carries the aura of the sacred, but in a perverted manner. There is a deep ambiguity in our cultural attitudes about money. On the one hand we take money and its acquisition very seriously, but on the other we tend to laugh at people who are anal-oriented, or even hold them in contempt. Gold is the color of feces, and Freud taught us to recognize that on an unconscious level money is equivalent to excrement. Money is a secular competitor to religious faith; the money system works only if people believe in it. This is especially true of "fiat" money which is not based on anything of physical value.

Your credit is good if you have credibility. Many religions prohibit usury; charging interest for loans of money is considered sinful. These ambiguous associations have to be repressed in order for the money system to be socially acceptable; but the repression is barely conscious, and it results in guilt so that the whole money complex is neurotic, rooted in the psychology of guilt. If people who want to make money are acting out of infantile forms of anal sexuality as they cherish filthy lucre, they do not really know what they are doing.

Many years ago the ancient Greek philosopher Aristotle distinguished between *oikonomia* (household management) and *chrematistike* (making money), which he recognized as an unnatural perversion. Since pure acquisitiveness, after one has a comfortable livelihood, has no real aim other than having, it is a desire without limits.

I have been deeply concerned about money for many years, but especially since our current president said he thought that climate change was a hoax and withdrew from the Paris Accords, the international effort to reduce carbon dioxide in the atmosphere. Many other people seem to follow his lead, but not necessarily because they have doubts about climate change. They share his desire to "make America great again." But if this is done by abolishing the Environmental Protection Agency so that economic growth has no regulation, they seem willing to sacrifice the only planet we have for the sake of money, and this outrages the environmental moralist in me.

Several years ago I wrote an imaginary dialogue called "The Demons Discuss Money." I will include the ending of it here. The speakers are three demons: Belial, Mammon, and Satan.

> Belial: I mentioned the importance of economic growth a few minutes ago. We see it as a process by which humans transform the substance of the earth into money. It works on every level, starting with simple agriculture. When we got farmers into the capitalist economy so they could sell their harvest, they soon exhausted the fertility of the soil by trading it for money.
>
> Mammon: And when they use up the natural fertility they have to buy artificial fertilizers, and this is another way for humans to turn earth's resources into money.
>
> Belial: Right! But our most diabolically clever stroke of genius was when we showed humans how to open the earth and extract its fossil fuel resources. The Creator may recycle, but we like to burn stuff. The energy generated by this burning has created the greatest wave of economic growth ever in the history of the earth. Our energy corporations are now making more money than any corporation has ever made. And that energy has supported a population explosion that is crowding out all other forms of life on the earth. Exponential growth is speeding up our ultimate plan.
>
> Mammon: But what if they use up all those fossil fuels? Humans are really addicted to oil.
>
> Belial: It does not matter. The burning of fossil fuels has generated enough pollution for us to achieve our plan. The climate is changing as gases given off by burning coal and oil trap the heat of the sun. But our energy corporations are successful in confusing humans about global warming. The earth is ours and as it gets warmer it will soon be a habitation suitable for us.
>
> Satan: We love a warm place. And with the power of money we have succeeded in thwarting the will of the Creator by spoiling the earth he created for humans

and the other creatures. We are moving toward the end of our game, and we will succeed.

My interest in money was sparked by Tom Greco at a Green Politics gathering in the late 1980s. His first book on the topic, *New Money for Healthy Communities*, was self-published in 1994, and he has since published two more on this topic. I studied the issue of money intensely and wrote some good papers on it but published them only in local newsletters. And I offered a course on money in our local community college. More importantly, when I was active in the Greens in the late 1990s I organized a LETSystem (Local Employment and Trading System) in Bangor which was sponsored by Michigan Land Trustees. We had about 50 members and there was vigorous trading, but not quite enough of a critical mass to survive. Later, in about 2008, I worked with a young city manager in Bangor to get another LETS started. We called it BETS, Bangor Exchange and Trading System, but it ended before it got fully started when the city manager moved to another city. These systems of mutual credit create community as

compared to using cash which buys personal independence. Bernard Lietaer has pointed out that the word community derives from two Latin roots: "*cum*, meaning together, and *munus*, meaning the gift, or the corresponding verb, *munere*, to give. Hence 'community,' = 'to give among each other'." Whether or not the official money system can be reformed, systems of community currency would help us evolve from a nation of money-grubbers to people who cooperate with their neighbors. And as they bypass the formal economy they do not contribute to growth in the market economy.

In 1995 I proposed that the Neahtawanta Center, in the Traverse City area, should devote an issue of their newsletter to community economics. They did that and I contributed an essay entitled "The Need for a Third Way in Economics." In addition to jobs and welfare payments for those who could not work, I proposed a third way of non-monetized subsistence activities that should be developed—the household economy. From Ivan Illich, I borrowed the term "vernacular" to denote cashless but productive activities in the household or community. We still use the word vernacular with reference to language learned at home in contrast to the language taught in schools, but originally it had a broader meaning which included whatever was home-made rather than purchased. We are losing vernacular activities because of what Illich called "radical monopoly," in which industrial products and professional services substitute for useful activities in which people engage or want to engage. "A radical monopoly paralyzes autonomous action in favor of professional deliveries." Perhaps even more problematic is the fact that as radical monopoly replaces vernacular activities many people lose the ability to think and do for themselves. Thus the market economy tends to replace the household economy which can only be recovered either by imaginative and original thinking or by sheer necessity when neither jobs nor welfare payments are available. The culture of subsistence is lost.

Recession, if not economic collapse, may be coming in the near future, and it would be tragic if people are so tied to their jobs that they are unable to imagine a future in which they could be effective in self-provisioning. The effects of global warming may already be felt in places where rainfall is either excessive or inadequate. But this is on top of many other forms of environmental degradation. And one of the most damaging is the destruction of a living topsoil by exploitative, chemically-dependent agriculture. Although chemical fertilizers can feed plants, the soil in which they grow is otherwise dead and will not produce without continual fossil fueled inputs.

The oceans, which are the ultimate sink for much of the pollution on land, are also becoming more acidic as the excess carbon dioxide in the atmosphere finds its way into the sea. Oceans are no longer a dependable source of food. In the longer term, as ocean levels rise with water from the melting of glaciers, millions of people will be migrating further inland from cities now just above ocean levels.

Still another persistent and virtually permanent pollutant that industrial societies are bequeathing to the post-industrial future is radioactive waste. My wife and I live about ten miles downwind from a nuclear power plant so we have been fighting to get it shut down for many years. It was scheduled to close in 2018, but for economic reasons that closure was postponed to 2022. The clean-up afterwards is a very expensive process, and as Hard Times come upon us, we are worried about how persistent the radioactive pollution will be.

This list of consequences of the current energy-intensive industrial modes of production could go on and on, but the most decisive problem will be the end of fossil fuels, and this will be a problem both if they are used up or if there is an ample supply. Long before the last barrel of oil is burned it is likely that the effects of climate change will be upon us. The J-curve of rising population growth followed the J-curve of rising energy use as fossil fuels made more food possible so that more people could live.

During my lifetime the global population has grown from two billion in 1930 to seven billion in 2012. Seen under the paradigm of economic growth, this was a great achievement; but when seen under an ecological paradigm, it is tragic because it exceeds the carrying capacity of the planet. At this point, anyway, the limits in energy resources no longer make that kind of growth sustainable. This was already obvious in 1977 to then-famous energy expert Howard T. Odum who argued that a new homesteading movement was needed to conserve energy.

There may very well be die-offs in some parts of the planet, mass migrations in other parts, and social chaos in many parts, all of which could add up to the collapse of civilization, as John Michael Greer has argued. Since human societies have not succeeded in slowing population growth in anticipation of diminishing resources, nature will balance population and resources with die-offs. At this point we do not know what the ultimate result will be. In the long run humans may join many other life-forms in the Sixth Great Extinction. (Of course a nuclear war, followed by a nuclear winter, in which the smoke and dust from blasts blocks out the sunlight, could also extinguish human life.) Or, since climate change takes time to become lethal, (my guess is at least 50 to 100 years), humans may use that time to challenge the forces of death and destruction and evolve policies that promote life. Temperatures are likely to rise as much as 4 degrees Fahrenheit by the middle of this century. Whether they continue to rise, and by how much, depends on what is done in the meantime to mitigate global warming. Mitigation is technically possible, and humans want to live; thus there is hope for a human future.

The Midwest is the most intensive agricultural region in this country, with more than two-thirds of the land devoted to crop production. It already has a longer growing season and warmer winters, but also increasing late spring freezes, more heat and drought in summer, and more frequent heavy rains and flooding, all of which complicate agricultural production. Tree fruit producers have been especially hurt by late spring frosts, while high nighttime temperatures have reduced corn yields between 2002 and 2012. These climate effects are likely to increase at least until the middle of the 21st century. After that, as temperatures rise, the effects will be worse unless serious efforts are made, on a global scale, promptly, to sequester the excess carbon in the atmosphere through organic farming and other techniques.

Raising Food to Slow Climate Change

Methods of organic growing were introduced in Chapter V above. Although the soil needs to be supplied with rock minerals or wood ashes or bone-meal, organic matter is the main fertilizer added to soil with which the organisms in the soil make nutrients available to plants. Chemical or synthetic fertilizers are to be avoided because they disrupt or damage the organisms in the soil. Anhydrous ammonia, as a source for nitrogen, is above all to be avoided because it emits nitrous oxide, the third major greenhouse gas, which has three hundred times more warming capacity than carbon dioxide. Methane is the other major greenhouse gas, 25 times more powerful than carbon dioxide, and potentially the most dangerous because it is released as tundra melts or as the ocean warms. It is also emitted by ruminant animals and in rice growing. Carbon dioxide is released from deforestation and excessive tillage, as well as burning fossil fuels, but these practices are well understood and can be avoided. The most immediate strategy is to avoid tillage for weed control, since it causes carbon to oxidize when organic matter is exposed to air. There are several strategies of no-till growing. On a gardening level, it can be accomplished with mulch. This is important because long-term studies reveal

The author mulching his garden

average losses of 328 pounds of organic matter per year per acre with plowing, whereas no-till methods show an average increase of 956 pounds of organic matter per year per acre.

It is necessary to increase organic matter in the soil because chemical farming practices have depleted it in soils. Fifty to eighty percent of the carbon in the soil has escaped into the atmosphere. Cropland, which should have around 5% organic matter, is down to 1 or 2%. Undisturbed prairie soils can contain 10 to 20% of organic matter, which was put there naturally by photosynthesis using carbon dioxide and water. Since over half the organic matter in soil has been lost, the soil can easily accommodate at least twice as much as still remains in it.

The need to mitigate emissions is urgent, but the reduction in burning fossil fuels is slow because people are accustomed to their energy-intensive lifestyles. Americans are not likely to give up their cars, which emit about 5.6 pounds of carbon in the form of carbon dioxide for every gallon of gasoline burned. Thus the more immediate strategy gains importance: the sequestration of carbon in plants and trees. But because these eventually rot and give off their carbon dioxide, the more durable sequestration is in humus in the soil. The formation of humus is enhanced by mycorrhizal fungi which secrete a protein called glomalin that builds humus in the soil and makes it more stable. This data is gleaned from a paper published by the Rodale Institute ("Regenerative Organic Agriculture and Climate Change") which argues that it is possible to sequester as much carbon as is emitted—eventually. It provides data to support this from studies in several countries, but it is dependent on a transition to regenerative methods of organic farming, which is slowly happening. The value of the Rodale paper, which is highly respected, is that it shows that global warming can be slowed so that other strategies to combat it can be developed. Many other studies corroborate the Rodale conclusions.

Still other possibilities for mitigating climate change are proposed, including simplistic technological solutions to get rid of atmospheric carbon as if it were a simple pollutant. Some of these techniques would try to capture the carbon and bury it. These must be opposed because carbon is a necessary nutrient for plant growth; but we must get it out of the atmosphere and into the soil from whence it came. The most efficient way of doing this is the most natural: photosynthesis. The preference for technological solutions over natural solutions implies a distrust of nature; this distrust applies also to organic farming where it is reinforced by vested economic interests that make money on agricultural inputs such as chemical fertilizers and pesticides. We can only hope that the power of organic farming to sequester carbon is given widespread publicity.

Other strategies can reinforce organic farming. One is from permaculture, which emphasizes perennial rather than annual food-producing plants. Trees have long been recognized as an efficient food source, but mechanization made annual crops easier. A book published in 1929 showed that trees, per acre, can produce food equal to cleared land. They can also grow on hilly land, have a longer growing season, and do not need tillage. Their deeper roots can better tolerate extremes in precipitation, and more trees should be planted as the climate changes.

A treetop of our enormous sugar maple

The wood in orchards and forests, which is 50% carbon, can be turned into charcoal when it is past maturity, so its carbon is stabilized, or it can be preserved as lumber. My son Karl, who lives in Detroit, has taught me a lot about biochar as he demonstrated how to make biochar on my farm and elsewhere. He is also working to organize an ecovillage.

The importance of planting more trees raises the question of whether there is enough land to do so. The answer is that there is adequate land, at least in this country. Millions of suburbanites and rural residents maintain almost 40 million acres in lawns. These lawns could gradually be converted to permaculture plantings and thereby help to raise food, while also sequestering carbon with perennials. Other food producing perennials are under development at the Land Institute in Salina, Kansas, or in process of rediscovery by horticultural explorers.

Another consideration that is taboo for policy-makers in this country, at least so far, is the process of deindustrialization after there is widespread recognition that fossil fuels can no longer be burned. The industrial food system is the biggest user of fossil fuels and eventually it will be curtailed.

The average family of four uses as much energy in the supermarket food they buy as in the car they drive. The alternative to the industrial food system is for people to raise their own. This is likely to begin in the back yard for household use, but eventually small-scale farming will continue to grow and also be supported by policies so that food can be made available to those unable to raise their own. More farmers markets and CSAs (community supported agriculture) are rapidly emerging. Although the Great Plains are likely to suffer the impacts of climate change before the Midwest states further east, they have enormous areas of land which could be resettled. At this point it seems that the ravages of global warming will move into the Midwest, and into Michigan, later than elsewhere. The Midwest, however, received a 37% increase in heavy precipitation between 1958 and 2012, while the Northeast received a 71% increase in that time.

My Major Community Activities and the Emergence of an Environmental Ethic

Most of my efforts in building community organizations grew out of the School of Homesteading. The School itself, of course, was also recognized by local media as a community organization. It had a specific location north of Bangor and was the place at which a variety of workshops and meetings were open to the public, often co-sponsored by Michigan Land Trustees and/or Organic Growers of Michigan. Although our last large class was in 1981, we continued to host two or three students each summer until 2001 when we moved off the farm and into our new house, so the School of Homesteading really functioned for a little over a quarter century.

The Kaufmans' farm of 101 acres is located just north of Bangor, Michigan. Each year between eight and ten young people interested in learning the arts and skills of low-technology subsistence farming come to live at their school. The term lasts from May 1 to October 31, and gives the students a chance to live in and be a part of the demanding life on a productive farm.

As I explained at the beginning of Chapter V, homesteading and organic farming were two sides of the same coin. My activities in the organic movement, however, continued for most of the rest of my life. All this is recorded in Chapter V and will not be reviewed here, except to mention that the talk I gave in early 2005 at the annual Organic Conference in East Lansing, "Organic Farming and the Organic Way of Life," was my first effort to consider the larger ethical issues implied in organic farming. These larger issues were developed a bit more in my book *Adapting to the End of Oil* and they were implicit in the off-grid house we built in 2001. But they did not yet take conscious form as an environmental ethic.

It was only in the writing of this book, as I reviewed my activities over the years, that I became fully aware that I was acting out an environmental ethic. As I reflected on what I did I became conscious of what I was thinking. The ethic that governs organic farming is really very simple: take, with gratitude, what nature offers, but do not force nature to give more with artificial fertilizers. As I thought

Solar panels, fifteen years after installation

about it, this same ethic governs energy use: take, with gratitude, the energy offered by sun and wind, but do not generate more by burning fossil fuels. Also implicit in my commitment to Michigan Land Trustees is the same ethic: use the land you need to live on, but do not seek to own or control more than is needed.

I should add here that the way reporters saw my activities as a unified environmental effort helped me to understand what I was doing. This was especially vivid in the picture showing the photovoltaic panels while the article with it reported on organic farming. Although these two kinds of activities evolved separately in my life, I was learning to see them as different aspects of a larger environmental ethic. The previous chapter suggested that the practice of organic farming preceded an ethical theory about it, and this is the case with the emergence of my environmental ethic. In that essay I also pointed to the view in process theology that "the world is God's Body," and that environmental concerns are helping us recognize ourselves as cells in that Body.

IN OUR OPINION

Living green

Look to Bangor – not Hollywood – for role models

Maybe a few Hollywood celebrities could learn a lesson from a Southwest Michigan couple.

We're talking about the celebrities who lecture us about our "carbon footprint" and how guilty we should feel for driving SUVs – just before they hop on their private jets to fly to Cannes, using more carbon fuel in a few hours than most of us will use in a year.

The environmentalist hypocrites – "do as I say, not as I do" – are getting harder and harder to take, and they're doing their cause more harm than good.

Not so for Maynard Kaufman and his wife, Barbara Geisler, of Bangor. They are environmentalists who practice what they preach. They heat their home by burning wood, not natural gas. They get electrical power from their own solar panels and wind turbines, not from the power company. They produce most of their own food, and what they buy comes from local farms.

They're hoping they can spread

Another unsolicited recognition of our environmentalism was an editorial in the Herald Palladium newspaper from Saint Joseph, Michigan. The editorial mentioned that we heated with wood, generated our own electricity, produced most of our own food, and were trying to develop an ecovillage which would be totally solar-reliant. (After the housing market collapse in 2008 that ecovillage project failed.)

Then, in 2015, I read a paper at a "Rooted and Grounded" conference at the Mennonite Biblical Seminary in Elkhart, Indiana, and as I prepared it I did try to articulate the religious basis for my ethic about land use in the face of global warming. Although I did refer to earth-centered spirituality from my book, *Adapting to the End of Oil*, I found myself returning to the Biblical story of creation with its mandate to till and keep the garden. This led to the affirmation of stewardship: "we are the stewards or managers of God's estate; we are responsible for its preservation." From all this I have to conclude that my environmental ethic is based on several strands in my thinking: a panentheistic understanding of the world as the Body of the Goddess, (even as it is modified by human actions), with earth-centered spirituality lending an aura of the sacred to the earth we are to use and preserve. If we see ourselves as cells in the body of the Goddess, we will not want to harm that body.

My activities in the Green Politics movement, and especially in the Transition Initiative which followed the local Green movement, were more explicitly based on the ethic articulated in Rob Hopkins' *Transition Handbook*, with its subtitle, *From oil dependency to local resilience.* Our local group sponsored "reskilling" events to help people remember food-raising skills along with discussions and talks on problems with energy use. We organized in 2009 and were the 49th group to get together in this country. Eventually there were over 130 Transition Towns in this country and nearly 500 worldwide. Since we began as a two-county "hub" we helped local towns develop active groups. Some of these are still active, but one thing we learned from Transition as a movement is the importance of timing. In this country, anyway, the emphasis on an "energy descent plan" came too early. People were not ready for it.

Although climate change is a global issue, the focus on it here has been mainly in the United States. This is appropriate because this country still emits the most carbon dioxide per capita. Until China, with a vastly larger population, displaced the United States as the highest emitter of carbon dioxide, we were the top emitter. China, which has high levels of air pollution in its cities, seems very concerned to mitigate carbon emissions. Less industrialized nations are burning less fossil fuels and may be more inclined to adopt cropping methods to mitigate emissions. The United States, as a capitalist country that idolizes money, may be the most reluctant to give up fossil fuels or move to cropping methods that could sequester carbon dioxide in the soil. As a wealthy nation with over 84% of its citizens considered over-consumers, we are the main problem. And it is exacerbated by the huge disparity of wealth since the 1% who are the richest create the largest share of greenhouse gases.

Despite my dark thoughts about the possible collapse of civilization, my life has continued with hopeful plans for our survival as humans. But Americans are still so exuberant that they do not seem ready to adopt the self-discipline we all need to learn. It is possible, and would be helpful, if changing circumstances would force us learn. A serious economic recession, if it could be seen as a clear manifestation of climate change, would be useful in waking people up to the fact that our way of life is not sustainable. Americans have generally ignored several versions of "limits to growth" books since 1970s, and so we are likely to suffer the consequences of limitless growth. We may learn from real life experience what we could not learn from science.

Afterthoughts on Environmental Ethics

Two considerations prompt me to rethink environmental ethics appropriate to our time. The first was expressed a few pages back and I will repeat that paragraph here: "During my lifetime the global population has grown from two billion in 1930 to seven billion in 2012. Seen under the paradigm of economic growth, this was a great achievement; but when seen under an ecological paradigm, it is tragic because it exceeds the carrying capacity of the planet. At this point, anyway, the limits of energy resources no longer make that kind of growth sustainable."

In other words, the growth in human population is stressing the planetary environment. Soils, oceans, and the atmosphere are all polluted and already curtailing the production of food for people, so that production now comes only by further damaging these natural resources. An example is deforestation and the burning of fossil fuels to increase food production, which add greenhouse gases to heat up the planet. This is the second of the two considerations: the growth of the human population is damaging the planet so less food can be produced as more is needed. And non-human life forms are crowded out.

Historically, our ethics in the Western world have always been humane—we have cherished the value of human life to such an extent that it has blinded us to the value of the non-human world. Our ethics are derived from our religion, which is the most anthropocentric in the world as God is manifest in human form. The natural world is valued, but it is not considered sacred. We depend on that world for our survival, and if it is seriously damaged human survival is threatened. Herein lies our quandary: how can we continue to promote a humane ethic when it is threatening human survival? Perhaps this is a time when human die-offs must be tolerated for the well-being of the planet. Perhaps we should no longer work to save human lives when there are already more than the planet can support. Thus a true environmental ethic would replace a humane anthropocentric ethic.

If my logic in the preceding paragraphs is correct, some practical consequences follow. First and most obviously, we must oppose and seek to discredit those among us, such as Catholics and many Evangelical Christians, who oppose birth control and contraception. The Biblical mandate to "be fruitful and multiply, and fill the earth and subdue it" may have been appropriate when humans were few on the earth, but now that the human population has grown exponentially and filled the earth, it is a dangerous mistake and totally inappropriate. At the same time we can support those groups and organizations that promote family planning and smaller families.

Other, harsher, consequences of recognizing over-population in a time of diminishing resources can be imagined. Should we refuse assistance to organizations that seek to feed the hungry or generally offer help to suffering people? The ethical basis for this may be that feeding the hungry rather than letting them die continues to stress the planet. Organic gardeners who make compost know that new life can emerge out of the death of the old. Death is part of the cycle of life and death. Should we seek to save lives when the next pandemic comes along? Or should we sorrowfully accept a pandemic as a natural cleansing?

I have added these "afterthoughts" several weeks after I thought I was done with writing this book. I was dissatisfied with the rather glib or superficial nature of the environmental ethic I had lived by. Although this ending may not be in harmony with the book as a whole, I will let it stand because it fits with the topic of this final chapter "Resisting Climate Change." And then, and then, some smart aleck, more radical than I, will come along and argue that we should not resist climate change but accept and affirm it as a necessary cleansing of the earth.

About the Author

Maynard Kaufman was born in 1929 and raised by Mennonite parents on a farm in South Dakota. After graduating from college he went on for graduate study in the Divinity School of the University of Chicago where he began writing his doctoral dissertation, *James Joyce and The Temptation of Modern Gnosticism.* His teaching career was at Western Michigan University from 1963 to 1987 where he began teaching courses in Religion and Literature and then switched to courses in Religion and Environmental Studies after having helped to start the new program in Environmental Studies.

In 1973 he was granted a half-time leave of absence from classroom teaching to conduct a School of Homesteading on a farm suitable for this purpose near Bangor, Michigan. When Organic Growers of Michigan was organized that same year he had his farm "Certified Organic" and was soon active in the organic movement. In 1991-1992 he was the co-organizer of Michigan Organic Food and Farm Alliance.

He has published many articles on food, farming, and energy issues, and in 2008 he published *Adapting to the End of Oil: Toward an Earth-Centered Spirituality.* In 2017 he co-edited *The Organic Movement in Michigan* with Julia Christianson.

In 2001 Maynard and his wife Barbara moved into the off-grid house powered by sun and wind they built on a part of their land so they could sell other parts of the farm and farm buildings to three younger organic growers. Thus they could retire from farming, but he still enjoys gardening to raise their food.

Acknowledgements

There are several people who helped to make this book possible. First is Julia Christianson, who had served as co-editor with me as we published *The Organic Movement in Michigan* in 2017. When I proposed to write this memoir she once again volunteered her computer skills and quite literally put this book together after I wrote the pages. She also corrected many of my errors.

My son Conrad, a professional artist and muralist in the Kalamazoo area, responded to my request for a cover. He had also provided insightful comments on the structure of some chapters. My wife, Barbara, is not only my first reader, but also the person with excellent literary judgment who advised me when I was unsure about what to include or exclude. My friend, the writer Paul Gilk, faithfully worked through each chapter with a red pen and corrected most of my mistakes. Any remaining mistakes are my own.

Finally, thanks to Wendell Berry for permission to reprint some of his poetry. Even more thanks are due for his persuasive agrarian writings that have shaped my life ever since he visited the School of Homesteading in 1974.

Photo Credits

All photos by Maynard Kaufman, except as noted:

Page 14	Photos of students picking green beans in the commercial garden and selling produce at the farmers market by Ardyce Czuchna-Curl.
Page 27	"Just Married" photo by Marion Leedy.
Page 33	Hull Family photo courtesy Greg Hull.
Page 45	Photo by Sally Kaufman.
Page 51	Sally Kaufman feeding maple syrup evaporator by Ardyce Czuchna-Curl, 1977.
Page 57	Photo by Marian Kaufman.
Page 59	Greens summer solstice ritual on our farm, by Maynard Kaufman.
Page 63	South Dakota farm by John Suderman.
Page 65	Stone pile in front of pond, by Maynard Kaufman.
Page 69	Swift Hall, used by permission from Terren Wein, editor of *Criterion*, a publication of the University of Chicago Divinity School.
Page 77	Swift Hall and Bond Chapel connected by cloister, by Maynard Kaufman.
Pate 83	Pseudo-medieval gargoyles on University building, by Maynard Kaufman.
Page 85	Harper Memorial Library, used by permission from Terren Wein.
Page 88	Nathan Scott, used by permission from Terren Wein.
Page 93	Soil Food Web illustration courtesy Natural Resources Conservation Service. https://www.nrcs.usda.gov/Internet/FSE_MEDIA/nrcs142p2_049822.jpg.
Page 96	Photo from an article by Richard Lehnert in *Michigan Farmer*, March 3, 1979.
Page 101	Sally Kaufman, a few weeks prior to her death, by Paul Gilk.

Page 105	Cover of *The New Farm*, January 1984. Photo credit: Mitch Mandel.
Page 107	Photo of Paul Gilk by Bob Seitz.
Page 117	Illustration by R. Crumb of women seeding, from the cover of the Summer 1977 issue of *The Co-evolution Quarterly*. Copyright © Robert Crumb, 1977. All rights reserved.
Page 129	Illustration by Penny Kelly from *The Elves of Lily Hill Farm*. Used by permission.
Page 134	Hazel Henderson's three layer cake, reprinted in *The Living Economy*, edited by Paul Ekins (Routledge Kegan Paul, 1986).
Page 144	Photo by Barbara Geisler.
Page 148	Sally and Maynard Kaufman, from an article by Tom Gettings in *Organic Gardening and Farming*, March 1975.
Page 149	Photo by Jon Towne, June, 2018.
Page 150	A portion of an editorial in the [St. Joseph, Michigan] Herald-Palladium.
Page 151	From a brochure promoting the Transition Initiative. Design by Conrad Kaufman.
Back Cover	Photo by Jon Towne, 2018.

Notes and References

Dedication

When Sally and I were married in 1962 she came with three children, Mary Michal (deceased) and Jonathan and Nathan, for whom I tried to serve as stepfather.

Karl was born in 1958 when I was married to Marian, and he visited us often.

Conrad and Adrian were born in 1963 and 1966 when I was married to Sally.

Chapter I: A Time of Transition

p. 2, "J. F. Powers," see my literary essay, "J. F. Powers and Secularity" in *Adversity and Grace*, edited by Nathan A. Scott, Jr. (Chicago: The University of Chicago Press, 1968), 163-181.

p. 2, ""Post-Christian Aspects," see my theological essay, "Post Christian Aspects of the Radical Theology," in *Toward a New Christianity: Readings in the Death-of-God Theology*, Edited by Thomas J.J. Altizer (New York: Harcourt, Brace and World, 1967), 345-364.

p. 2, "work in study and field," This is an example of the kind of integration, as opposed to division of labor, proposed by the anarchist, Peter Kropotkin, in his book *Fields, Factories and Workshops Tomorrow* (Harper Torchbooks, 1974) p. 26.

p. 4, "Paul Shepard," see a couple of his books, *Man in the Landscape* (New York: Alfred A Knopf, 1967) and *The Tender Carnivore and the Sacred Game* (New York: Charles Scribner's Sons, 1973).

p. 4, "John Cobb," see his book *Is It Too Late?: A Theology of Ecology* (Beverly Hills: Bruce, 1971).

p. 5, "Ronnie Cummins," quoted in *Organic Struggle* by Brian K. Obach (MIT Press, 2015), p. 41.

p. 6, "another essay I wrote," "The New Homesteading Movement: From Utopia to Eutopia," in *Soundings*, (Spring, 1972, Vol. LV, No. 1) 63-82. Reprinted in *The Family, Communes and Utopian Societies*, edited by Sallie Teselle (Harper Torchbooks, 1972), 63-82.

p. 6, "attracted the attention," see my essay in the book edited by Thomas J. J. Altizer, mentioned above, and Harvey Cox, *The Feast of Fools* (Cambridge: Harvard University Press, 1969) p. 196. See also John B. Cobb, *The Theology of Altizer* (Philadelphia: Westminster Press, 1970), 164-175.

p. 10, "limits to growth books," see Donella Meadows, et. al. *The Limits to Growth*. (New York: Universe Books, 1972). A small book by Edward Goldsmith and his editorial associates of *The Ecologist* Magazine, called *Blueprint for Survival*, (Signet Books, 1972) is another book on limits.

p. 17, "Horses," by Wendell Berry in *Collected Poems, 1957-1982* (San Francisco: North Point Press, 1985) 225-227.

p. 21, "articles appeared," see Tom Gettings, "The New Homesteading Schools" in *Organic Gardening and Farming* (March, 1975).

p. 23, "My friend, Ken Dahlberg," see his book, *Beyond the Green Revolution* New York: Plenum Press, 1979).

p. 23, "critics of technology," see E. F. Schumacher, *Small is Beautiful* (New York: Harper Torchbooks, 1973) and Ivan Illich, *Tools for Conviviality* (New York: Harper and Row, 1973).

p. 26, "critique of schooling," see Ivan Illich, *Deschooling Society* (New York: Harper and Row Harrow Books, 1972).

p. 27, "the 1970s were the back-to-the-land decade." According to Charles E. Little and W. Wendell Fletcher in "Buckshot Urbanization: The Land Impact of Rural Population Growth" (*American Land Forum*, Vol. II, No.

4 (Fall, 1981) 10-17), "the 1980 census showed that between 1970 and 1980 population in non-metropolitan areas grew at a rate of 15.19% as compared to a 9.8% growth rate in metropolitan areas. This is the statistical back-to-the-land movement. In fact, this growth in rural population is not limited to counties adjacent to cities, but leapfrogged to non-adjacent counties where the rate of growth was 14.2% as compared to 17.5% in adjacent counties. But both rates of rural growth are higher than the 9.8% rate of urban growth. This kind of rural growth has been called 'buckshot urbanization.' About three-fifths of the non-metropolitan counties in the country are growing at a rate faster than metropolitan areas."

p. 28, "Schell's book, see Jonathan Schell, *The Fate of the Earth.* (Stanford University Press, 1982)

p. 28, "Ernest Callenbach," see his book, *Ecotopia* (Berkeley: Bantam Books, 1979).

Chapter II, Back to the Farm

p. 42, "the example of Wendell Berry," see his poem in *Leavings* (Berkeley: Counterpoint, 2010,) 96.

p. 50, "densely wooded ancient forest," see Robert W. Emmert, *Bangor, Our History in Photographs* (Published by the author, 2004) Chapter One.

p. 51, "tapping trees" see Helen and Scott Nearing, *The Maple Sugar Book* (New York: Schocken Books, 1971).

p. 52, "permaculture," see Mark Shepard, *Restoration Agriculture: Real World Permaculture for Farmers* (Austin: Acres USA, 2013).

p. 53, "corn, the killer of continents," See J. Russell Smith, *Tree Crops* (New York: Devin Adair, 1950).

p. 53, "the Land Institute," The Land Institute was co-founded by Wes and Dana Jackson in 1976 near Salina, Kansas. It has garnered international support for the effort to develop perennial versions of our annual grains.

Chapter III: The Deep Roots of my Environmentalism

p. 60, "Transition," see Rob Hopkins, *The Transition Handbook: From Oil Dependency to Local Resilience.* (White River Junction, VT: Chelsea Green Publishing, 2008).

p. 60, "Green politics," See John Rensenbrink, *The Greens and the Politics of Transformation.* (San Pedro: R. and E. Miles, 1992).

p. 60, "my book," see Maynard Kaufman, *Adapting to the End of Oil: Toward an Earth-Centered Spirituality* (Xlibris, 2008).

p. 66, "numinousity," see Rudolf Otto, *The Idea of the Holy* (New York: Galaxy Books, 1958). See also Mircea Eliade, *The Sacred and the Profane* (Harper Torchbooks, 1959).

p. 67, "Loomer," see Edgar A. Towne, "Theological Education and Empirical Theology: Bernard M. Loomer at the University of Chicago" in *Journal of Religion* 2004. 212-233.

p. 67, "Whitehead," see Alfred North Whitehead, *Process and Reality* (New York: The Humanities Press, 1929). 34.

p. 68, "emphasis on relationship," see Charles Hartshorne, *Reality as Social Process* and *The Divine Relativity* (Boston: Beacon Press, 1953, and New Haven: Yale University Press, 1964).

p. 69, "how process thinking led to environmentalism," see Ron Engel, "Making the Earth Covenant at Chicago," in *Criterion* (Winter, 2008), 11-17.

p. 71, "Mennonites as excellent farmers," see C. Henry Smith, *The Story of the Mennonites* (Newton, Kansas: Mennonite Publication Office, 1950), 320-323

p. 71, "Mennonites in Russia," see Karl Stumpp, *The German Russians: Two Centuries of Pioneering* (Bonn: Atlantic-Forum, 1967).

p. 72, "Mennonites and agrarian life," see S. Roy Kaufman, *Healing God's Earth* (Eugene: Wipf and Stock, 2013).

Chapter IV: A Doctoral Dissertation on James Joyce

p. 76, "Nathan Scott," professor of Theology and Literature in the Divinity School and eventually my doctoral dissertation adviser. He published books such as *The Broken Center* (1966), *Negative Capability* (1969), and *The Poetics of Belief* (1985).

p. 77, "Preston Roberts," a student of Bernard Loomer who retained him to start a new field of study called Religion and Art in the Divinity School in 1948. Pres published only a handful of excellent articles (some of which are discussed in the text) and was my major professor and adviser until he suffered a mental breakdown in about 1968.

p. 79, "The Redemption of King Lear," see essay by this title by Pres Roberts published in *Renascence* (Vol. 26, Issue 4, Summer 1974).

p. 82, "David Grene," see his book *Of Farming & Classics* (University of Chicago Press, ca. 1975).

p. 86, "modest interest among some theologians," see note to p. 6.

p. 87, "typology of tragedy," see Preston Roberts, "A Christian Theory of Dramatic Tragedy," in *The Journal of Religion* (Vol. xxxi, no. 1, January, 1951), 1-20.

p. 87, 'the modern story" quoted from "The Redemption of King Lear," op. cit., 191.

p. 89, "only one doctoral student" Josephine Donavan at the University of Wisconsin.

p. 89, "Gnosticism as a Christian heresy," see Rudolf Bultmann, *Primitive Christianity* (New York: Living Age Books, 1956, p. 163. "The Gnostic myth recounts—with manifold variations—the fate of the soul. It tells of its origin in the world of light, of its tragic fall and its life as an alien on earth, its imprisonment in the body, its deliverance and final ascent and return to the world of light."

p. 90. "Symbolic consciousness," see Norman O. Brown, *Love's Body* (New York: Vintage Books, 1963) p. 200.

p. 90, "Nathan Scott," see his *The Broken Center* (1966), p. 21.

p. 90, "antitheist," see Bernard Benstock, *Joyce-Agains Wake* (Seattle: University of Washington Press, 1965) p. 107.

p. 90, "death of God," see Thomas J. J. Altizer, *The Gospel of Christian Atheism*, (Philadelphia: Westminster Press, 1966), p. 21.

Chapter V: My Role in the Organic Movement

p. 91, "National Gardening Association," (180 Flynn Avenue, Burlington, VT 05401).

p. 91, "Paul Hawken," see his book, *The Next Economy* (Holt Rinehart and Winston, 1983) 123-124.

p. 92, "Wendell Berry," see *Farming: A Hand Book* (Harcourt, Brace Jovanovich, 1970). See also his *The Long-Legged House* (Audubon/Ballantine Book, 1972).

p. 93, "Elaine R. Ingham," see *Soil Biology and the Soil Food Web* (presentation at MOSES Organic University, 2015). Another very large book that is focused on the recovery of the agrarian vision in the context of our still dominant mode of industrial food production is *Fatal Harvest: The Tragedy of Industrial Agriculture* (Washington: Island Press, 2002). It is lavishly illustrated and includes essays by over fifty of our most competent agrarian and organic writers.

p. 95, "Mary Applehof," see *Worms Eat my Garbage.* (Flower Press, 1982).

p. 99, "David Pimentel," see his article in *Bioscience* (Vol. 28, No. 12, Dec. 1998).

p. 104, "The first was in 1982" at the University of Florida, where I read a paper called "Visions for the Future of Agriculture," published in *Agriculture, Change and Human Values, Vol. I* edited by Richard Haynes (University of Florida, 1982) 67-86.

p. 104, "The second, in 1984" was at the University of California at Santa Cruz, where I read a paper called "From Domination to Cooperation," published in *Global Perspectives on Agroecology and Sustainable Agriculture*, Edited by Patricia Allen and Debra van Dusen (Santa Cruz: Agroecology Program, 1988) 75-82.

p. 105, "The third conference, in 1986," was at Michigan State University, where I read a paper called "The Pastoral Ideal and Sustainable Agriculture." It was published in *Sustainable Agriculture and Integrated Farming Systems*, edited by Tom Edens (East Lansing: MSU Press, 1985) 219-228.

p. 105, "In 1974 we were featured," in an article, "The New Homesteading Schools," by Tom Gettings, in Rodale's *Organic Gardening and Farming* (March, 1975) 120-123.

p. 105, "And in 1984 I made the cover of The New Farm," see "Evolution of a Small Farm," by Paul Gilk, in *The New Farm* (January, 1984) 22-25. His most recent book was *Picking Fights with the Gods* (Wipf & Stock, 2016).

p. 107, "I wrote a book," See note to p. 60 above.

p. 109, "articles on how organic farming could mitigate climate change," "Agrarian Revival at the End of Cheap oil," in *Green Horizon Magazine* (Fall, 2008), 10-12; "Raising Food in a Changing Climate," *MLT Newsletter* (Spring, 2013); "Carbon Sequestration, Naturally," in *Green Horizon Magazine* (Fall-Winter, 2014); "Hubris or Humus," *Farming Magazine* (Spring, 2015) 8 and 68.

p. 109, "Liberty Hyde Bailey." One of the many books Bailey wrote he called *The Holy Earth* and an edition was recently published by the Museum with a forward by Wendell Berry.

p. 109, "hydroponic vegetables as organic," see Ronnie Cummins, "Organic Standards: What's Next?" in *Acres USA* (February, 2018), p. 5 and 90.

p. 110, "illegal certification of hydroponic growing," see Mark Kastel "Cornucopia Calls for Investigation of NOP," in *The Cultivator* (Winter, 2016) 2-3.

p. 112, "love of money," see I Timothy 6:10 in the Bible.

p. 111, "There are other proposals, see The Night They Drove Organic Down—https://www.keepthesoilinorganic.org/night-they-drove-organic-down.

Chapter VI: Food Systems: Sacred, Profane, and Demonic

p. 116, "food systems," see Dietrich Knorr, (editor), *Sustainable Food Systems* (Westport, Connecticut: The AVI Publishing Co., 1983.

p. 117, "the great historian of religion," see Mircea Eliade, *Patterns in Comparative Religion* (Meridian Books, 1967), Chapters VIII and IX.

p. 119, "remember how Faust," see the dramatic version by Christopher Marlowe, *Doctor Faustus*, edited by Sylvan Barnet (Signet Classic, 1969).

p. 119, "remember how Jesus," see Matthew 4:1-10.

p. 120, "Norman O. Brown," see his *Life Against Death* (Vintage Books, 1959), p. 240.

p. 120, "Paul Tillich," see his *The Protestant Era* (Phoenix Books, 1950).

p. 122, "demonic corporations," see Brewster Kneen, *From Land to Mouth: Understanding the Food System* (Toronto: New Canada Publications, 1993), p. 45. See also Chapter I on "distancing."

p. 123, "fascism," see Thom Hartmann, *Unequal Protection: The Rise of Corporate Dominance and the Theft of Human Rights* (Emmaus, PA: Rodale Books, 2002), p. 190.

p. 125, "E. F. Schumacher," see his *Small is Beautiful*, (Harper Torchbook, 1973).

p. 126, "Rudolf Steiner," *Spiritual Foundations for the Renewal of Agriculture* (Biodynamic Farming and Gardening Association, 1993). The book was originally published in 1924 as *Lectures on Agriculture.*

p. 127, "A Gospel According to the Earth," article by Jack Hitt in *Harper's Magazine* (July 2003).

p. 127, "Creation Spirituality," see Matthew Fox, *Original Blessing: A Primer in Creation Spirituality* (Santa Fe: Bear and Company, 1983)

p. 128, "New Story," see Thomas Berry, *The Dream of the Earth* (San Francisco: Sierra Club Books, 1988).

p. 128, "Wendell Berry," see his *Farming: A Hand Book* (Harcourt, Brace Jovanovich, 1970), p. 3. See also Berry's *The Long Legged House* (New York: Audubon/Ballantine Book, 1971).

p. 129, "elves and fairies in the garden," see Penny Kelly, *The Elves of Lily Hill Farm: A Partnership with Nature* (St Paul: Llewellyn Publications, 1997).

Chapter VII: Resisting Climate Change

p. 131, "one theological essay," see note for p. 6 above.

p. 132, "From utopia to eutopia," see my essay on the New Homesteading Movement, in note for p. 6 above.

p. 133, "Scott Burns," see his book, *Home, Inc.: The Hidden Wealth and Power of the American Household* (Garden City, New York: Doubleday & Co. 1975). See also Helen and Scott Nearing, *Living the Good Life* (New York: Schocken Books Inc. 1970.

p. 135, "Karl Polanyi," see his book, *The Great Transformation* (Boston: Beacon Press, 1957), p. 57.

p. 139, "Tom Greco," see his self-published book, *New Money for Healthy Communities* (1994).

p. 139, "Systems of mutual credit," see Bernard Lietaer, *The Future of Money* (London: Century, 2001) p. 182.

p. 140, "community economics," see my essay: "The Need for a Third Way in Economics," in *Synapse* (Spring, 1995, No. 31), 3-5.

p. 140, "vernacular," see Ivan Illich, *Toward a History of Needs* (New York: Pantheon Books, 1978), p. 39.

p. 142, "Howard T. Odum," See his article "The Ecosystem, Energy and Human Values" in *Zygon: Journal of Religion and Science,* (June 1977), p. 132. See also the book by Howard T. Odum, *Environment, Power and Society* (New York: Wiley-Interscience, 1971).

p. 142, "collapse of civilization," see John Michael Greer, *Dark Age America: Climate Change, Cultural Collapse, and the Hard Future Ahead* (New Society Publications, 2016), chapter 2.

p. 142, "nuclear winter," see Daniel Ellsberg, *The Doomsday Machine* (New York: Bloomsbury, 2017). At the end of the book Ellsberg compares climate change to the nuclear threat as equally destructive.

p. 143, "The Midwest is the most intensive," see Laura Lengnick, *Resilient Agriculture: Cultivating Food Systems for a Changing Climate* (New Society Publishers, 2015), chapter two.

p. 144, "increase in organic matter with no-till," see Albert Bates and Toby Hemenway, "From Agriculture to Permaculture," in *State of the World, 2010* (Washington, DC: Worldwatch Institute, 2010), p. 52.

p. 145, "formation of humus is enhanced." The reference to mycorrhizal fungus is from the paper by the Rodale Institute, "Regenerative Organic Agriculture and Climate Change," (2014), p. 7.

p. 145, "many other studies corroborate," see, Lal, R., et al., *The Potential of U. S. Cropland to Sequester Carbon and Mitigate the Greenhouse Effect.* (Boca Raton: Lewis Publishers, 1999). Also, see Thomas Goreau, et. al., editors, *Geotherapy* (CRC Press, 2014), pp. 37ff. *Geotherapy* is a long book of about 600 pages over 30 chapters by different authors, including at least ten articles that clearly demonstrate different ways to sequester excess carbon dioxide into the soil

p. 146, "A book published in 1929," see J. Russell Smith, *Tree Crops: A Permanent Agriculture* (New York: Devin Adair, 1950).

p. 146, "biochar," see *Biochar for Environmental Management*, edited by Johannes Lehmann and Stephen Joseph (Earthscan, 2009).

p. 147, "horticultural explorers," see Eric Toensmeier, *The Carbon Farming Solution* (Chelsea Green Publishers, 2016).

p. 147, "ravages of global warming will move into the Midwest," see Laura Lengnick, *Resilient Agriculture: Cultivating Food Systems for a Changing Climate* (New Society Publishers, 2015), chapter two.

p. 147, "almost 40 million acres in lawns," see Douglas Tallamy, *Bringing Nature Home* (Portland: Timber Press, 2007), p. 32.

p. 151, "Transition Initiative," see note to p. 60.

p. 152, "limits to growth books," see Donella Meadows, et. al., *The Limits to Growth: A Report for the Club of Rome's Project on the Predicament of Mankind* (New York: Universe Books, 1972). This was the first of the Limits books by the Meadows, to be followed by two more book with updated data in 1992 and 2005.

p. 153, "human die-offs must be tolerated for the well-being of the planet." The ethical issues raised here were discussed several years ago in a book edited by George Lucas and Thomas Ogletree, *Lifeboat Ethics: The Moral Dilemmas of World Hunger* (Harper Forum Book, 1976), and good arguments were made for feeding the hungry. But that was before the issue of climate change emerged.

p. 153, "Biblical mandate," see Genesis 1:28.

CPSIA information can be obtained
at www.ICGtesting.com
Printed in the USA
LVHW041839200819
628309LV00015B/1197/P